D0228959

A
Gardener's
Dozen

CONTENTS

FOREWORD

The publication in book form of a series of broadcast talks linked to a common theme produces a stimulating, indeed fascinating, symposium. Twelve distinguished horticultural writers, all lovers of plants and knowledgeable of them, write of gardens, and particularly their own gardens, each taking a different month of the year: and, through ingenious planning, not necessarily the month which most favours the plants with which one mostly associates each writer.

If the book is read straight through, which it is difficult to resist doing, the difference in the contributors' style of writing – or rather of composing their talks – gives an added charm to the book.

Alternatively it is a book that can last the strong-minded reader for a year, if he reads about each month at the outset of that month.

Most readers will have heard each of the contributors talking, or lecturing; and this can impart an extra vividness and naturalness so that one can almost hear the writer talk as one reads.

There is much to be learnt from the book but, more important, the opinions expressed are often such that one is tempted agreeably to dispute them from one's own experience, perhaps more fortunate, perhaps less so, than the writer's.

The beauty of a garden in winter, with its tracery of trees, and its shape and balance clearly to be seen: the burgeoning of early spring: the culmination of flower that comes for most of our gardens in late spring or early summer: the sad vividness of

A Gardener's Dozen

Anne Scott-James

Alan Bloom

John Sales

Peter Coats

Christopher Lloyd

Hugh Johnson

Lanning Roper

Beth Chatto

Graham Stuart Thomas

Wilfrid Blunt

Valerie Finnis

Roy Lancaster

BRITISH BROADCASTING CORPORATION
in association with
the Royal Horticultural Society

This book is based on the Radio 3 series of
talks devised and produced by Pamela Howe,
Radio Talks Producer at the BBC Network
Production Centre, Bristol

The Publishers would like to thank
Michael Joseph for permission to include an extract
from 'The Garden' by V. Sackville-West

Published by the
British Broadcasting Corporation
in association with
the Royal Horticultural Society
35 Marylebone High Street
London W I M 4AA

ISBN 0 563 17726 8

First published 1980
© the contributors 1980

Printed in Great Britain by
Jolly & Barber Ltd, Rugby
Bound by Dorstel Press Ltd,
Harlow, Essex

autumn, with its glorious colours and fading falling leaves: all these are here brought to mind to arouse our recollections and stimulate our gardening ambitions. So perhaps the winter fireside may be best suited to the full enjoyment of this fascinating book.

Lord Aberconway
President of the
Royal Horticultural Society

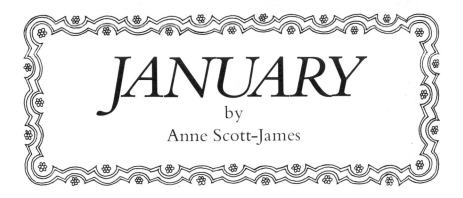

JANUARY

by

Anne Scott-James

My garden, which is a cottage garden in the country, is not at all spectacular. Except in June, when the roses are in full swing, it is not a garden of bright pictures and dramatic views, but a garden where there is always something out. It's a personal garden, where there are lots of odd corners full of treasures, and secret places with small clumps of flowers in bloom if you know where to look for them. This kind of garden has plenty of faults, I know, including a tendency to spottiness, but it has one great merit – it gives pleasure to its owner in every month of the year. January is no exception. Even in a hard winter with frost and snow I can stalk out in my gumboots and be sure of finding early bulbs and small herbaceous plants in bloom, and probably shrubs as well, though shrubs admittedly run more risk in frosty weather. I always try to have a few flowers out in January by the front door, to cheer up our visitors as well as the family.

My favourites among the January flowers are the absolutely trusty ones which *always* come out, whether it's cold or mild. Wholly reliable in my garden is the small iris, *Iris histrioides* 'Major', which will come up through thick snow. It is about five inches tall, a madonna-blue iris with gold and white marks on the falls. Two or three bulbs will quickly increase into a good clump, and they don't resent it if you fork them over by mistake in the summer and have to replant them. One warning – they like good drainage, which they get naturally in my chalk garden, but if you garden on heavy soil, it would be best to plant them in a raised bed, or to dig in some coarse grit underneath the bulbs. This is the only iris which always comes up for me in January, because the scented *Iris reticulata* waits until February, and I cannot persuade the most famous of the winter irises, *Iris unguicularis*, to flower before March, although I have tried several different forms. Some of my gardening friends pick them at Christmas, but although I've given them a sunny wall, they hold back. There are no absolute rules in gardening; every garden has its own peculiar behaviour. I must mention one other January iris which I love: the tiny yellow *Iris danfordiae*. The trouble with this is that it flowers perfectly in its first year, and then disappears, for the bulbs break up into tiny bulbils, but a famous alpine gardener has given me a tip to prevent this. He told me to plant the bulbs eight to ten inches deep, which is amazingly deep for such little bulbs, so I planted a handful deep down last autumn as an experiment, but I won't know until next January if I am going to keep them going.

Another group of plants which give me unfailing pleasure in January are the hellebores. The first to open in my garden is always *Helleborus atrorubens*, and the first flowers usually come out just before Christmas. The clumps produce many stems of dusky-red nodding flowers, several flowers to a stem, between Christmas and March, or even April. Before the end of January, they are joined by pink, green, and white forms of *Helleborus orientalis* – the pink is my favourite. All can be picked for the house, if they are plunged in water at once and kept in a cool room – some gardeners say you should dip the stems first in boiling water to seal them. They need protection from the wind and mine grow in the shelter of a large clump of laurels. A hard night frost will make them go limp and bow their heads to the ground, and you think they're ruined; and then you go out at midday to find them sitting up, quite recovered. Laurels, incidentally, though hideous as a hedging plant, because they clip badly, make splendid protective clumps in an informal bed, or in a wild or woodland garden.

The Christmas rose, *Helleborus niger*, is not so satisfactory in my garden. I have two clumps in bud now, looking rather bedraggled, and the leaves are pock-marked with holes, this plant is caviare to slugs and the flowers get soiled by rain and snow. It really needs protecting with cloches, but I find these so unsightly in the flower garden that they spoil the pleasure. Frankly, the Christmas rose is not easy to grow, though dazzling in its pure white beauty when successful.

Several of the green-flowered hellebores come into bud during January and are already a pleasure to look at, though they won't be fully out for a month or so. I grow, among others, *Helleborus corsicus*, with large, green water-lily flowers, *Helleborus foetidus*,

2 A clump of *Helleborus corsicus*

with branches of smaller flowers, and the dwarf *Helleborus viridis*, which grows wild in the woods near my cottage. All have elegant, deeply-cut leaves to pick for the house if you are short of flowers. *Helleborus corsicus*, I am afraid, needs staking, for a fall of snow will break the hollow stalks which have to support heavy heads of flowers. I have recently seen another hellebore which I covet, but have not yet acquired; it has apple green flowers and is called *Helleborus odorus*.

Two other flowers are January near-certainties. One is the winter aconite. Some gardeners find these difficult, but I think it is because they buy the dry little corms which are on the market in the autumn. Aconites should be moved while growing, so try to get a clump from a friend while it is still in flower, or soon after flowering, and move it quickly so that it can carry on growing in your garden. You must certainly get it before it has shed its seeds, so that you get the benefit of the seedlings. Aconites grow best where there is sharp drainage, but I have seen them flowering abundantly in a great variety of places, with or without lime in the soil. They seem particularly happy under chestnut trees. My other standby is not so well-known – a periwinkle called *Vinca difformis*, with flowers which are white in the winter, and mauve later on. It spreads profusely by layering.

I like to pick a mixed posy of all these January flowers, perhaps including a pretty weed like celandine, and to put them in a china jug on my desk. There is usually a lingering stem or two of the floribunda rose called 'Rosemary Rose' to add to the bunch, and an early primrose or polyanthus, and some winter pansies, and a sprig of rue or santolina from the herb garden.

Usually there are some shrubs in flower this month, but of course a really harsh spell of weather can damage the flowers. My winter-sweet, or *Chimonanthus praecox*, sometimes gets knocked about by the frost and snow; it is only in a mild year that I get plenty of flowers. This can be a disappointing shrub, slow to flower after planting and far from frost-proof, but in a good year the scent is so exciting and overpowering that one forgives all its shortcomings. V. Sackville-West described it perfectly in her poem, *The Garden*:

> Still may you with your frozen fingers cut
> Treasures of Winter, if you planted well;
> The Winter-sweet against a sheltering wall,
> Waxen, Chinese and drooping bell;
> Strange in its colour, almond in its smell.

The winter-flowering cherry, *Prunus subhirtella* 'Autumnalis' is out now, looking rather mushy in the garden but thick with buds which will open fresh and clean indoors. It is best planted against a dark background, perhaps a holly tree. Some of the mahonias are in flower. 'Charity' is nearly over, but that excellent cultivar called 'Buckland' is coming out and sometimes *Mahonia aquifolium*, not due until March, makes an early appearance in January.

I am also learning to value skimmias in winter, for they are perfectly hardy and their evergreen leaves retain a high gloss in the worst weather. It is essential to have both male and female forms, so buy them only from a nursery where they are properly labelled. *S. japonica* 'Rubella' is one of the best male varieties, 'Foremanii' is prominent among the females. If you don't grow both sexes, you will get no berries.

These are the only small flowers I can count on this month, but in a mild January there may be many more – perhaps the first snowdrops, probably *Anemone blanda*, perhaps a stem or two of pulmonaria. In addition to various blue forms of pulmonaria, I have a white form I am devoted to called 'Sissinghurst White'. I am not very good at naming snowdrops, which is a complicated matter, but I believe my earliest to be *Galanthus elwesii*, a tall snowdrop with wide glaucous leaves and green markings on the flowers. I also have masses of double snowdrops, a favourite old cottage flower, which have spread into my garden from a piece of wasteland where there was once an old cottage, now pulled down.

Then there are usually a few freak flowers which have no

business to be out, but put in an appearance at odd times of year when they feel like it. One of these is the shrubby wallflower called Mr Bowles's wallflower, because he grew it in his famous garden at Enfield, but its correct name is *Erysimum linifolium* 'Bowles Purple'; it has charming cruciform mauve flowers.

Another more unusual but very pretty shrub which is in flower is *Coronilla glauca*, which flowers all the year round. It has small yellow pea flowers and delicate glaucous foliage. There is a variegated form, but it is less hardy. The winter jasmine has been flowering since November and is usually good for a week or two in the New Year. You may wonder why I don't mention one of the finest winter shrubs, the richly scented witch hazel or *Hamamelis mollis*, but that is because my soil has too much lime for it. I would grow it if I could. The most beautiful hamamelis I have seen is an American clone called 'Arnold Promise' of which there is a plant at the Royal Horticultural Society's garden at Wisley – a splendid clear yellow flower with no hint of orange in it. I believe it is not yet commercially available, but will be propagated in due course. Another shrub which I have not mentioned is forsythia, for I am not very fond of it in the garden, finding its manner of growth uninteresting or even gawky. But I have one large plant in an inconspicuous spot in the garden for cutting in January and forcing into flower in the house. Sprays cut at New Year and brought into a warm room should be in flower in about three weeks.

Some of the best January shrubs have a beauty which has nothing to do with flowers: a beauty of leaf or bark or structure, which shows up best in winter. The dogwoods have splendid crimson stems now; I always cut them down to a foot or two from the ground in March to get plenty of the young wood which colours best. There is a magnificent Scots pine in the garden next door, which glows fiery red if there is a gleam of winter sun, but in summer I scarcely notice it. And I enjoy the bare shapes of trees and shrubs. I like to admire through my kitchen window the spidery skeleton of *Cotoneaster horizontalis*; and I make excuses for visiting a friend in the village who has that fascinating, eccentric shrub, the corkscrew hazel, *Corylus avellana* 'Contorta'. The great Victorian gardener, Canon Ellacombe, found the first recorded plant in a Gloucestershire hedge, and later gave a scion to his friend E. A. Bowles.

In our own garden, we take pride at this season in our yews. Running across the boundary of our back garden we have some seventy feet of yew hedge with a gap in the middle to give a view of the rolling farmland beyond, now bare and brown and furrowed by the plough. This hedge is in poorish soil and started slowly after planting. Then, one summer, it galloped away when I fed it with dried blood – a smelly job but worth it, for it is now

3 The statue of Diana flanked by yews

4 & 5 The changing face of the Acteon statue in winter and summer (opposite) under 'Rose Maigold'

vigorous and five feet high. We also have an arch of yew sheltering a statue of Diana, and four Irish yews flanking the central garden path. I try to brush the snow off the yews after any heavy fall, because a weight of snow can snap the branches of evergreens and do a lot of damage. Indeed the kindest thing one can do for a garden in January is to go out early with a twiggy broom and brush the snow off every plant which looks overloaded.

Another pleasure in this season is one's modest collection of pots and statuary – not antiques, alas, because I have no gift for picking up valuables at country sales for a song – some buyer more cunning than I has always got there first. But at the top of a rickety flight of steps I have two Italian terracotta baskets filled with *Iris histrioides*; I have one or two Italian stone statues which look comic

just now with rakish hats of snow; and I have a pair of lions, made of composition stone, over which I am trying to train some ivy. I want their bodies to be covered with ivy, with just their fierce heads poking out, and I think it is going to work. Ivy, like most climbing plants, is a slow starter; it dawdles for a year or two growing a root system, and then starts to climb fast. You may think that all these statues sound inappropriate in a cottage garden and so they are, but my husband brought most of them with him when he left a large house and garden which had formerly been his home, and now they are a valued part of our garden scene. To me, gardening is as much a matter of associations as of planting and cultivating, and I always remember who gave me a plant, or when and where I collected it wild, often in some favourite place.

Of course there are many more fine winter plants than those I have mentioned. These are the ones I grow myself, and am enjoying now. But other gardeners will have their hollies this January, their sarcococcas with small scented flowers, their winter heathers, the yellow stems of willows, perhaps *Garrya elliptica* with its long tassels, and plenty more. Those who garden on acid soil have a much wider choice of trees and shrubs with winter interest than I have in my chalk garden. Some of the maples are outstanding, especially *Acer griseum*, with a highly polished bark which flakes in winter to reveal an orange skin beneath. The plants I want to add to my garden, if I can find space, are one or two golden conifers: perhaps a golden Lawson cypress like the variety called 'Hillieri'. They would soften the somewhat sinister quality of my Irish yews.

This lack of any golden conifers is something I must put right, but I am well off for variegated broad-leaved evergreens and find them very cheerful on a grey day.

The best of the daphnes, to my mind, is variegated – *Daphne odora* 'Aureomarginata', with evergreen leaves edged with gold. I have several variegated ivies, including the small-leaved 'Gold-heart', and a variegated coronilla. And there is the fine elaeagnus with brilliant green and yellow leaves, *Elaeagnus pungens* 'Mac-ulata', which in winter seems to be growing in a pool of sunshine. Its leaves grow quite dull in summer, so it is a true winter plant. It is excellent for cutting, and I like it mixed with sprays of box.

I must say a word about vegetables. The pigeons are so pestilen-tial in our district that I have given up growing greens like sprouts and broccoli, which grow above the ground, and I concentrate on roots and leeks. I have still got plenty of leeks in our vegetable bed. We love them in cheese sauce, or in soups, or as a salad with a vinaigrette dressing, and when the ground is frozen hard I pour warm water over them so that I can fork them up. Leeks, together with onions and broad beans, are the oldest of all cottage veget-ables, and have been grown in cottage gardens for many centuries. Near the house, so that I can get at them in the worst weather, I

6 The bold pattern and branching growth of *Hedera helix* 'Goldheart' enliven a winter wall

always grow one or two clumps of Welsh onions, which are like giant chives, but do not disappear in winter. When neither chives nor spring onions are available, Welsh onions can be chopped up to decorate soups and flavour those rather dull winter salads.

Another winter essential is parsley, which I protect with cloches, but thyme, rosemary, and sage usually survive in the open. When we have had a good apple year, I hope still to have some Bramley apples in store, though most surplus fruit goes into the deep freeze.

But the garden in January is not just a matter of present pleasures. There are plans to make and jobs to do. It is a good time, when the garden is comparatively bare, to muffle up and walk round slowly, with a notebook, planning changes in design. I want to get more plants right up near the house for winter enjoyment, for some of mine are too far away. In really bad weather the only way of seeing flowers may be through the windows. I must also decide on the removal of some of my shrubs. I like a crowded garden, but mine has become thoroughly overgrown, particularly with shrubs, and there will have to be some elimination. I think it is better to take out a whole shrub here and there, rather than to prune them all, perhaps in the process destroying their natural shape.

And of course it is the time for ordering seeds. Now I am an early bird with this job and usually send in my modest vegetable list long before Christmas, in case the varieties I want run out of stock. But I have not yet ordered my flower seeds, and this will pass a pleasant evening by the fire. I no longer heat my greenhouse – it's too expensive – so I shall not need seeds for early sowing under glass. But I shall want some sweet peas for sowing in the unheated greenhouse later on. I shall order a few frilled sweet peas in my favourite colours, and also a few of the old-fashioned pre-Spencer sweet peas with small flowers but an amazingly strong and heady scent. If we get a mild spring I shall sow the sweet peas direct into the open ground, but if the soil is icy I find it better to start them in pots. I buy most of my biennials, like sweet williams, from a garden centre in the spring, because biennials take a lot of labour, but I do grow my own wallflowers from seed because when you buy them as plants, you get too much top-growth and too little root. So I shall order wallflower seeds, probably a general mixture, with an extra packet of the colour called Blood-Red.

The rest of my seed order will be hardy annuals. Dwarf nasturtiums in a jewel mixture; that charming salvia called clary; lots of *Lavatera* 'Loveliness', which is an annual mallow with large pink trumpet flowers in July and August; and certainly some cornflowers. I want these in blue only and resent the mixed packets sold by so many seed firms. Who wants a pink cornflower? Not I. And I shall order some candytuft, as I have a small new area of paving which looks naked and I want to establish candytuft in the cracks.

I'd like to recommend one annual, which I shan't need to order as I have plenty of it and it sows itself from year to year the charming little yellow-and-white flower called the Poached-Egg plant. Its correct name is *Limnanthes douglasii*, and it was first collected in North America by the Scottish botanist, David Douglas, who sent back so many conifers from America which are now widely grown in Britain. He died young, poor man, collecting plants in Hawaii, where he fell into a wild-bull pit.

Whether there will be any outdoor work this month depends entirely on the weather. If there is a mild spell it would be a good idea to prick over the flower-beds and work in some general fertiliser. Like most gardeners, I thought my garden was too dry in the autumn to give it its usual autumn mulch, and it is going to need a lot of feeding and conditioning this spring. I also want to tidy up the leaves and fallen branches and general débris, a job which better gardeners than I finished before Christmas. One job I always do in January, if there's a week without frost, because I loathe it and like to get it over: I water all the brick and gravel paths with simazine weedkiller. I never use weedkiller on the beds, because I don't like the stuff, and I prefer to weed by hand, but on paths I find it essential. Watered on in January or February, there are no weeds at all for a year.

Usually, January is a pleasant month for me in the garden, because it is not physically hard (my back creaks more than it used to when I was younger). But there is much to look at, small treasures to pick for the house, and plenty of the best sort of gardening, which is in the mind.

FEBRUARY

by

Alan Bloom

Like most gardeners, I regularly prowl round after Christmas for the first sign of spring. When young it was the sight of aconites and snowdrops which cheered me, but over the past twenty years I've made a six-acre garden in which to grow the widest possible range of hardy perennials. And it's the first of these to flower which my prowling now seeks out by way of a bonus. I've known mild winters when aconites are cheekily showing up on New Year's Day, but so will the Japanese *Adonis* 'Fukujukai', and with flowers four times the size. Usually in February it's full open to display its glistening greenish-yellow anemone-like flowers, only a few inches high but making a brave splash against the backcloth of cold soil. And by the end of the month, another even larger-flowered adonis will be showing amid its ferny leaves. This is *Adonis amurensis* 'Plena'. Both prefer light open soil, not too dry, as does the lovely *A. vernalis* which flowers in April–May, and has a shorter dormancy period. But by February, I can often find a score of spring harbingers, braving the cold east winds which usually set in about Candlemas Day, there to remain till the second of May, as the old saw goes.

By February, unless under deep snow which seldom comes in East Anglia, the hellebores are often at their best. *Helleborus niger*, the Christmas rose, which I've never known to live up to its name without artificial aids, is making a splash of its white saucers. But it's a tricky plant, liable to sulk; and, maybe because it's temperamental, we all keep on trying to please or appease it. If plants can be induced to produce a good summer canopy of leaves, keeping the soil beneath cool, you can then expect a good show of flowers in winter. The earliest plum-reds, *H. atrorubens* and *abchasicus*, are much more accommodating. Of the two I prefer *abchasicus*, because it holds its canopy of dark green leaves for most of the winter, and is a little taller. Hellebores are notoriously promiscuous for interbreeding, so much so that true stocks of some species are now difficult to find. But no matter, for there's a wealth of hybrids, and under the name *Helleborus orientalis*, raised from seed, you could have a dozen plants, from palest pink to deepest maroon and claret red. Some are charmingly spotted within the petalled cups, and all will be reliably perennial in some shade. They're not soil fussy and can be left alone for years and years, even if deprived of an annual mulch to which they will respond rewardingly. I have a dozen or so named species and I'm not really bothered if they're botanically true or not. Years ago I selected two outstanding seedlings and, by dividing them every three years, ultimately decided to name them. Because they epitomised so much of what I felt for them, flowering so bravely in February and March, I chose 'Heartsease' for one name, and 'Winter Cheer' for the other. But I may never live long enough to name and share others I have selected, to increase by the same means; at least they'll be an incentive as well as models for longevity.

I'm pretty sure that one parent is *Helleborus colchicus*, which in most seasons has splendid year-round leafage and will often flower late in the year as well as early spring, with light purplish-pink flowers. But long life doesn't apply to all hellebores. We may have three February-April annual displays of the rather floppy-habited *H. corsicus*, or its hybrid *H.* × *sternii* with *H. lividus*. Both have clustered heads of pale apple-green to creamy-white flowers on two-foot stems; but thereafter one has to rely for replacements on seedlings which are often self-sown.

On the north side of an evergreen shelter belt I have two large island beds, designed specially to show something in flower from

8 An island scree bed with stone-built walls provides interest all the year round

February to November. They're six to eight yards across but nearest to the evergreens is a narrow path, so that in mainly shaded soil I can grow early flowering plants. Those usually in flower in February include not only hellebores, but no adonis because these like a more open position and lightish soil, and along the path I look out for pulmonarias opening their tiny bells. The first is *angustifolia* 'Azurea', intensely blue on six-inch sprays, followed by the even dwarfer 'Munstead Blue'. Much more robust is the early flowering 'Highdown', in which the blue flowers turn to pink on fading. Pulmonarias are so easy to grow, with blues, pinks, near-red, and white flowers, and some have prettily spotted or margined leaves and flower from February to May.

One or two pulmonarias have to be relegated to wilder parts of the garden for being somewhat too exuberant. These include 'Bowles Red', but those with the prettiest leaves, such as 'Pink Dawn' and 'Argentea' give pleasure all summer long wherever they're seen. I must have a score or so different kinds, and even this may be well short of the variations in existence.

I wish I could grow hepaticas well, but the double-flowered

forms, especially, seem to sulk. Indeed the double blue seems to be pining for some stimulant I've so far failed to provide, for I have a group half the size I began with twenty years ago. It is such a charmer, even if it grows only a few inches high, and the flowers are no bigger than a sixpence. The double white I've never found, and the red is also languishing. The singles of *Hepatica triloba* are a little happier in my soil, which is of neutral acidity, but I really must try lime to see if they'll respond. The correct name for *triloba* is now *nobilis*; and *transsilvanica* now applies to *Hepatica angulosa*. These are easier to grow, and at six inches are a little taller and later to flower. 'Loddon Blue' makes a good show of light-blue flowers in early spring but the blue of the now rare 'Ballard's Variety' is quite outstanding.

It's always a source of wonderment to me how the earliest flowers and bulbs brave the cold spells of February and March. They appear almost regardless of frost and snow; and even if, having come into flower, winter has another fling, they take little notice of it. This is all the more surprising when most of them grow only a few inches above the cold earth, and it applies to the wealth of primroses which may cheekily open in February. Most of mine are cultivars originating from the wild primrose, or from the purple *Primula juliae*. One of my favourites is *P. vulgaris sibthorpii*, which not only makes a splash of lilac-pink, when others are only making preparations to flower, but usually flowers in autumn too. And, unlike some, it never seems to suffer from drought or red spider, which afflict several of the more highly bred or modern varieties. At any rate, my group of *sibthorpii* were planted ten years ago, and now no soil can be seen between the plants because of the growth they've made; and still they flourish, as does the wine red with the name Blutenkissen.

The purple-red *Primula* 'Wanda' is probably the only cultivar to survive in almost every garden. Thirty years ago, I had about twenty others, but so often stocks became decimated by summer droughts, often combined with attacks of red spider which are so hard to defeat.

The doubles suffered most, and now I'm reduced to two of these – the white and the lilac – and not many named singles. This may well be because one tends to forget what has given pleasure in early spring by the time summer comes with its wealth of flowers and the war on weeds. But from luck rather than any special care, I have a large drift of 'Blue Riband' back again after a long lapse. This, too, flowered last autumn but then it was purple. Now, in its normal period, it is back to violet-blue and looks very well next to one which has a jack-in-the-green collar and deep red flowers, flecked white on the petal tips. It's a selection of my own and I named it 'Ariel'. Speaking of weeds, I have a very ambivalent attitude towards one which often opens its first flowers in February. Celandines have real charm at this time of the year, and I'm loath to grub them out unless they menace the survival of plants to which precedence must be given. Weeds are sometimes defined as plants in the wrong place, but here Celandines were in their natural habitat before I made the garden, and I've no intention of denying their right to co-exist.

I don't have a rock garden as a piece of mountain landscape with rocks and boulders. To my mind such a construction would be totally out of keeping in a more or less level garden which is barely a hundred feet above sea level, and forty miles inland, with no natural stone other than flints. These I have used extensively, not in the traditional way of building flint walls, but so as to show the most attractive face of each stone with as little cement visible as possible. Time and patience with a good selection of stones is all one needs to build flint walls which are effective and pleasing to the eye. What slopes I have are terraced by this means, and, apart from a flint garden shelter, I have a raised bed for alpines, with only a few rocks showing between the plants it contains. By late February, the first of the Kabschia saxifrages are glinting, along with the bright carpets of *Saxifraga oppositifolia*. Soon the yellow drabas will appear, and so the long succession of alpines continues till autumn as a source of constant interest. And even in winter one may see flowers on that charming silver-leaved white daisy,

9 Alan Bloom building with flint at Bressingham Hall

Chrysanthemum hosmariense, and the lilac *Erysimum* 'Constant Cheer'.

In February the heather garden often makes one of its periodic displays. The buds on the *Erica carnea* varieties, which have been waiting since autumn, open in their many shades of pink, as well as white in such masses that one scarcely notices the dead flowers on groups of summer-flowing ericas and callunas, which should not be clipped off until February-March. These are the lime-haters, but *Erica carnea* and *mediterranea* are not fussy. This garden I can scarcely include as mine, for it was my son Adrian's idea, and he planted it as an adjunct. He's also keen on conifers, and these not only set off the heathers but are used in my garden as well, as specimens here and there. Sadly, some have grown too large, and if I tend to put off from year to year the necessity of grubbing one out, I still know it remains condemned; the longer I postpone, the larger the space it will leave me to fill with something else.

28

Conifers are the continuity links in a garden. It's a vital function, for they change but little in colour from one season to another, and in the darkest depths of winter they stand out like sentinels, alive and colourful, while the plants which promise the flowers are resting and waiting for the returning sun's warmth. Conifers are not my speciality, but I would miss them terribly, especially in winter. Their appeal is not only for foliage colour and effect. Given reasonably light soil, those that are fairly slow growing have such a wonderful range of form: carpets and cushions, mounds, domes, minarets, towers, steeples, pyramids, and even obelisks, are all included in their shapes, with colour variations thrown in as a bonus to their grace or symmetry. To a less striking extent, the same applies to heathers, although the space left, when an outgrown group of heathers is taken out, makes one wonder how or when the stark void will be filled again.

As a specialist in perennials, my plantings over the past twenty years have taken relatively little account of shrubs. For example, my *Daphne mezereum* died of old age a few years ago, and I still haven't replaced it, despite its value for earliest spring. Not so with the mahonias – *M. japonica* and others – which show up so brightly, with their huge clusters of yellow against the dark green background of a shelter belt. The witch hazel, *Hamamelis*, also yellow, is flowering well this year, little puffs hugging its leafless stems. And there's the ubiquitous forsythia, which I nearly always forget to prune hard back, as I should, once flowering is over.

Wintersweet, or *Chimonanthus fragrans*, flowers no better now, as a shrub flowering against a west wall, than it did before I moved it from a more open position. But the deliciously scented viburnums – *fragrans, bodnantense, burkwoodii* – flower profusely and regularly, with their heads of pinkish to pure-white, waxy flowers, and await warmer weather to open out.

I'll go along with the statement Valerie Finnis makes in her November chapter that a garden should be a home for plants; and even if I give pride of place to perennials, I'm finding spaces too for several more shrubs, especially dwarf kinds and those that flower in early spring. Shrubs associate much better with low-growing perennials rather than with the taller, so-called herbaceous plants. In with dwarf shrubs one can also grow early spring-flowering bulbs and corms, including such cheerful little beauties as *Cyclamen coum* and its forms, along with the irises of the *reticulata* type, and chionodoxa and crocuses. All these, and there are lots more, are reminders that even if winter returns with renewed icy grip, as it often does in February and early March, spring, none the less, cannot be far away.

Having over 100,000 visitors in my garden between Easter and Michaelmas, on days when I prefer to be an engine-driver giving rides on the Nursery railway, causes a few extra problems. The greatest is the wear on the grass walks, and for this there seems to be no reliable remedy. But for me it stands out like a sore thumb because worn patches never recover from one season to the next, in spite of returfing or seed sowing in autumn. I once tried a special plastic string netting for this purpose. It had to be pegged down so that the grass could grow through it, but the lawn mower was soon in violent conflict with it and it all had to be torn up. Perhaps a sprinkling of pulverised bark would be worth trying. In any case I intend using some as an experimental mulch to keep down the weeds and hold in summer moisture. There were no annual weeds when I carved the beds from the grass sward in making the garden between 1957 and 1962, but most of the usual enemies have since sneaked in.

If extra paving is laid in some of the worst affected places, the turf beyond its new limit soon begins to wear as well. Very little of the work that goes into my garden is done with the visitors in mind. It never has been, because my aim has always been to grow the widest possible variety of worthwhile and interesting plants to the best of my ability. Perfection in cultivation, harmony, and completeness, is like a 'will o' the wisp'. But I can't but keep on trying to reach it, any more than I can resist collecting additions to the variety I have already. Every summer, during the period of maximum growth, I go round, with a clip-board, bed by bed, making notes of improvements that could be made, including groups in need of moving or replanting.

Last year, my notes covered seventeen foolscap pages, because although some visitors had said the garden had never looked so good, I was far from satisfied. In some parts, the soil had become poached, calling for quantities of peat and sharp sand to be dug in. I began regrouping as early as August. I've gone in more strongly for segregation – fewer alpines as frontal groups to taller perennials, and kinds with little more than botanical interest reduced and relegated, to some extent, to less fertile beds; and, of course, a resolution to keep shrubs in more compatible surroundings.

Harmony must be studied, not only regarding colour, but time of flowering as well as effective contrasts. I try to intersperse spiky subjects, such as sidalceas, verbascums, and cimicifugas, between others having a more level or rounded habit when flowering – such as heleniums, phloxes, and day lilies. Colours seldom clash, but though I love to see blues and purples next to yellows, and pinks and reds next to whites and creams, the permutations on this theme are infinite. The fierce reds and magentas of some phlox or hardy geraniums can clash, but the white and pale blue of such as scabious and agapanthus – can enhance the most violent clashes to give delightful harmony.

Moving groups can be tricky, often leading to a chain reaction, if one decides the best site for a subject is already occupied by something else, for which another space has to be found. Once the process begins, there's no telling when it will end, with the feeling, if it ever comes, that all are just where they should be. Having so often made extra work for myself I didn't foresee, I've learned to ponder, to hesitate and change my mind, if need be more than once, in keeping to a rule not to move a group until I know where there's an available space. Spaces are a bit of a gamble. In the autumn I try hard to take account of what can be safely replanted then, without risk of having too many vacancies to fill in spring. The gamble is that, with many new additions needing a home, as well as moving or replanting kinds best left till spring, there could be too few spaces left for them when the time comes. There could likewise be too many to fill.

My general rule is to plant as early as possible in autumn the kinds that flower before midsummer, and leave late summer and autumn flowering kinds till spring. Any variations on this are made from experience, including trial and error, or success and loss. I can truthfully say that my love of plants has been my prime motivation – often transcending business considerations. It was so while I was a schoolboy, and even when I began as a master nurseryman in 1926. But I'm willing enough to admit that, even if I like giving plants away to some people, I also enjoy propagating those I believe are scarce or worthy of wider distribution: especially plants like the lovely double white *Trillium grandiflorum* 'Flore Pleno', which took me fourteen years from nine original plants before I had enough for a few to be sold. This is the extreme example, perhaps, but there is spice for me in backing my judgment of a good plant and then working up a stock, and I've usually several such subjects under my care and up my sleeve.

It may be a weakness of mine to be a discontented gardener in one sense at least. But this must surely be a healthy attitude, for it means that one is always on the look-out for possible improvements as well as worthwhile additions to one's collection. This discontent has made me go in for a sizeable raised peat bed, and plan a smaller raised bed of a suitable size in which to grow a variety of sempervivums and other tinies preferring minimal fertility. But to those who say, 'It's all very well for *you* to indulge your love of plants on such a scale, but what about *me* with a pocket handkerchief garden?' I have a stock reply. It's that perennials exist in such infinite variety that, with a careful selection, miniature beds can be contrived in quite small gardens and will become a source of joy. It's all a matter of scale and sensitivity.

It's when February comes with its slowly increasing daylight hours that I probe around for signs of renewed growth, especially on some of my treasures. And I'm happy when some are ready to dig up and divide, or whatever, to give me a pleasurable, absorb-

10 February snow at Bressingham Hall showing up the shapes of the trees

ing job for an hour or two after tea, even if the cold drives me to the warmth of my small heated greenhouse. And if I hear a blackbird then, trying out his voice nearby, I can wax quietly sentimental about spring coming, aware only of its joy and promise, beguiled into forgetting two offsetting factors. One is that spring brings a crescendo of work, and some headaches are inevitable. The other is that the sight of fading daffodils causes me a stab of regret, because I've been too busy once again to stand and stare, listen and smell, as often as I'd intended.

February for me is also a month for jobs I enjoy which lie outside my speciality of Hardy Perennials. I have for example an affection for pelargoniums and coleus which are neither hardy nor perennial. I usually prefer to pot up the few hundred rooted cuttings of pelargoniums, including the so-called geraniums, on my own, after tea or at weekends. And as soon as the January-sown coleus are ready to prick off in the heated greenhouse, this too is a pleasurable job. And I marvel that such fragile seedlings have within their tiny green leaves, at this stage, the capacity to produce such a gorgeous, intricate pattern of leaf colour later on. This wonder applies also when sowing seeds. Each kind, even those as small as fine dust, have within their microscopic shells all the properties and characteristics with which its evolutionary development has endowed it. It reminds one that we humans are part of nature, for the means by which we come into the world is basically no different from that of plants which reproduce from seed.

Back to the pleasure in handling plants, I can usually find seedlings to prick off, from seeds sown in summer. Some seeds of hardy plants are best sown in autumn to winter outside for natural spring germination. Others which need less time, can be sown from February to April. But there are a few, such as the Pasque Flowers *(Pulsatilla vulgaris)* and *Primula rosea* of which seed is best sown as soon as possible after it is ripe. If these are pricked off in autumn, frost may lift them, to leave their fragile roots exposed to dry spring winds and it is therefore best to leave them alone till renewed growth is imminent.

As a boy, I grew vegetables before I gravitated towards flowering plants. But now the only eatables I like to tend personally are rhubarb, strawberries and tomatoes. The latter I tend as babies, pricking them off, and potting them up to planting stage. It pleases me to see the lusty response they make first to careful handling and then to the special soil mix I concoct for them. And speaking of soil, there is a special smell, I find, to freshly dug soil in early spring. It is very faint, but it has a different, somewhat evocative odour, to soil sniffed in summer or autumn.

All I have to do with strawberries at this time of year is to sprinkle sulphate of potash between the plants, and then with a flat tined fork held at a low angle, turn over the top two inches of soil, so that the feeding roots will benefit, and the family can feast when summer comes.

But rhubarb is more special, because for me it is a year-round fruit, vegetable though it may be. My father, a devoted gardener, selected this clone from seed fifty years ago, and I have kept it going, valuing it highly as did he. My rhubarb bed yields its bright red stems for the first stew in February four years out of five, and provides my daily breakfast dish until October. From then, freezer reserves keep me going till Christmas, and clumps placed under the greenhouse bench, fill in the gap till February. I might well tire of strawberries if they were available all year round, but not this rhubarb, which I really think should be named 'Charles Bloom'.

One final thought comes to mind about being a discontented gardener, since my father was also one of these, in the sense I mean. It may be something of a paradox, but what I believe, is that real enduring joy or delight or whatever in gardening, comes largely in proportion to the thought and effort one puts into it. In working in with nature, always aiming for perfection yet knowing this will never be achieved, one is always stimulated into fresh efforts, and into experimenting. It is the act and the art of cultivation which then becomes a reward in itself, with successes as bonus and failures as a further challenge, one willingly accepts.

11 Spring catkins: *Alnus sinuata*

MARCH

by

John Sales

According to the calendar, spring begins at the vernal equinox around 21 March. But in a climate as varied as ours, such a rule of thumb won't do for the gardener. Independent of the date, we each receive our personal signal, however irrational, for the departure of winter. For some it may be the crocuses, for others the almond blossom or the forsythia; for me it's something between the bursting of the hawthorn buds – the 'bread and cheese' of my schooldays – and the arrival of primroses; not the occasional maverick blossom of winter but the full flowering of this our most welcome native.

The common primrose is a valuable garden plant both under shrubs and naturalised in rough grass. It's curiously tolerant of the common weedkiller, paraquat. I once visited a garden where spraying with paraquat was the sole method of weed control among shrubs. This is not a practice that appeals to me particularly but the result was interesting. After two or three years the ground was covered entirely by moss and primroses! The rose-pink form also flowers in March; and at Blickling Hall in Norfolk, under the ancient oriental planes, it and the common primrose sow themselves in a variety of intermediate colours. Seventeenth-century herbals described many varieties of *Primula vulgaris*, including several doubles, and a renewed interest has been shown in them recently. But perhaps the singles are the best garden plants, especially the lilac pink *P. v. sibthorpii* mentioned by Alan Bloom last

month. It flowers freely in cool places among shrubs providing it
escapes the ubiquitous sparrow which pecks out the buds almost
before they form; I find I have to protect all my primroses and
polyanthuses with black cotton.

The modern large-flowered F_1 hybrid primroses that one buys
as flowering pot plants don't persist long in the garden and are
better treated as showy bedding plants. A later primrose called
'Old Port', whose name aptly describes its deep colour, is truly
perennial. It grows well at Rowallane in Northern Ireland, where
the cool, equable climate is ideal for primulas. I wouldn't be
without the old cottage garden primrose known as 'Wanda' and in
my garden its crimson purple flowers are having a trial run among
the glaucous young shoots of *Sedum spectabile*, which will cover its
withering leaves later.

One advantage of being Gardens Adviser to the National Trust
is that, with cunning, I can arrange my garden visits to see the
arrival of spring more than once. By beginning in Cornwall and
travelling from south-west to north-east, it is possible to follow
the season across the country. But when does spring begin for the
gardener? Poets have written at length on the subject but our
admirable Advisory Service of the Ministry of Agriculture spurns
any such emotive term as 'spring'. It brings us right down to earth
by referring to the 'growing season': that is when the soil temperature at a depth of 300 mm (1 ft) is above 6°C (43°F), about the right
minimum for root development of grass and many evergreens,
bulbs and early herbaceous plants. It would, for example, be rash
to transplant evergreens unless the soil could be expected to
remain above 43°F for at least three to four weeks, so that new
roots can quickly penetrate the soil. The average date on which
this soil temperature is reached varies by as much as two months
from the third week in February in Cornwall, to near the end of
April in Northumberland and the Lake District. Apart from
coastal areas which are ahead by a week or two, the arrival of
spring progresses in these terms from west to east and from south
to north. For a large part of central and southern England the last

week of March is the critical date; so if you're thinking of moving any evergreens now, it would be safer to wait. Of course there are many local factors which affect this general trend, altitude, soil type, shelter and aspect all have an effect and, within a short distance, flowering dates can vary by as much as two weeks. The sheltered terraces at Powis Castle, near Welshpool, which face steeply south-east to catch the sun, show that these principles have been understood for centuries. Much of the fun of gardening lies in finding the right place for each plant and every garden, however small, has a range of habitat, part dry and part more moist, part sunny and part cooler.

12 The garden terraces at Powis Castle, a property of the National Trust

In Devon and Cornwall, gardens often nestle into wooded valleys to take advantage of the shelter they provide and are situated near the sea to avoid frost. Obviously these are gardens for early spring and March is not too soon for a visit. With lime-free soil and high rainfall, they're ideal for rhododendrons, a vast and interesting group of plants. All too often the whole genus is shrugged off as 'not nice' by gardeners who are unfamiliar with it or who may be intimidated by its complexity.

To some extent rhododendrons are like aspidistras, bergenias and Monkey Puzzles; they bring about extreme reactions. But how any gardener can dismiss such diversity of habit and foliage, and colour lasting for eight months of the year is difficult to understand. My view of plants is catholic by choice as well as by necessity. There are few bad plants; they nearly all have a use somewhere, but not in every garden. On the other hand, some gardeners are better able to envisage the ultimate effect than others. Indiscriminate and undisciplined planting is likely to fail as much in the rhododendron wood as in the herbaceous border.

A first principle for successful gardening is to grow plants which suit the site; to work with the conditions rather than against them. Along the west coast, given shelter, the moisture and warmth enables the large-leaved rhododendrons to grow to perfection. The sight of large bushes of R. macabeanum, R. grande and R. magnificum, with leaves up to a foot and a half long, flowering in March is worth the journey to Cornwall and even to the west coast of Scotland. The exotic effect is unique in British horticulture. But they need space to be seen at their best, and a rare case of where sufficient has been afforded is at Mount Stewart in Northern Ireland where a vast group of R. macabeanum is viewed across the drive.

Hardy enough further east, are forms of the tree-like R. arboreum, which towers to thirty feet in many gardens, forming enormous sprawling clumps bearing characteristically narrow pendulous leaves and compact flower trusses of white, pink and red. There are superb groups of the hybrid known as

1 A mixed posy of January flowers

2 Terracotta baskets planted with *Iris histrioides* and pots of snowdrops by a pair of composite stone Lion statues

3 A corner of Adrian Bloom's heather and conifer garden at Bressingham Hall

4 Above right: A carpet of blue *Scilla sibirica* at Hidcote

5 Right: The superb evergreen *Mahonia japonica*

6 & 7 Above: The highly desirable *Magnolia stellata*. Below: A border of polyanthus, showing the flower to its best advantage

'Russellianum' or 'Cornish Red' at Killerton in Devon. For the smaller garden perhaps the most reliable of March-flowering varieties is 'Praecox', a hardy plant produced over a century ago by crossing *R. ciliatum* with *R. dauricum*. Rosy-purple flowers cover the whole of this neat evergreen bush, and if the first are frosted often more will follow.

March in the south-west also brings camellias, both the hardy *Camellia japonica* types, which are legion, and the equally hardy *C. × williamsii* hybrids such as the semi-double pink 'Donation', which, unlike the japonicas, has the sense to shed its dead flowers. These shrubs are hardy further north and east, here they flower later, but are not suitable where late spring frosts are prevalent. In the most sheltered gardens of Cornwall they can grow even the tender and spectacular *C. reticulata* outside but even there it needs an unusual spell of frost-free and calm weather to see these enormous flowers undamaged.

Almost every self-respecting west country garden has its Himalayan *Magnolia campbellii*, the giant so-called Pink Tulip Tree, none more so than Lanhydrock in Cornwall, where magnolias are something of a speciality. Throughout Devon and Cornwall these noble trees rise to forty feet or more, making a crick in the neck an occupational hazard for garden visitors in March. The sight of a tree bearing many hundreds of enormous goblet-shaped flowers against a blue sky is unforgettable. At the little National Trust garden at Sharpitor, near Salcombe, accident or design has placed a specimen below a high terrace wall, affording us the rare pleasure of a close view of the waxy pink flowers.

I live on the cold inland edge of the Cotswolds where spring comes no earlier than in East Anglia and late spring frosts are common. Our soil rules out rhododendrons and our sharp continental climate shrinks leaves of other shrubs to half the size of the same species in Cornwall. March-flowering plants in this climate are those capable of responding quickly to comparatively short periods of warm weather, to complete their annual life cycle before their competitors get started. In spring, soil warms from the top downwards and shallow-rooted plants respond first, especially those with a store of pent-up energy in the form of a bulb or a corm.

Although crocuses are at their best here in March, I have a conviction that they belong to February. My best winter flowerer is *Crocus laevigatus* 'Fontenayi'. In poor soil and a hot sunny site it produces a succession of pale-lilac flowers, striped darker on the outside, from December to February. Whenever the snow melts there they are and with a little sunshine they soon show their yellow throats. Crocus corms are delectable to mice but not so scillas, which also seem immune to birds. As their common name, squill, suggests, the bulbs are toxic but the true squill poison comes from a different plant. The soft, darker blue stars of *Scilla bifolia* come early in the month, followed by *S. sibirica* which has a green tinge to its brilliant porcelain blue. Both are dwarf and spread freely by self-sown seedlings. Perhaps the most valuable is a showy form of *S. sibirica* called 'Spring Beauty' which, being taller, is ideal for giving early colour among shrubs and for naturalising in grass.

At Hidcote, *S. sibirica* makes a carpet of blue among the cut-down fuchsias, soon to grow up to hide the withering foliage of the bulbs. Closely related, but with a white eye to enliven the flower, is the Glory of the Snow, *Chionodoxa luciliae*. A few bulbs put in three years ago are spreading quickly among primroses under a large 'Nevada' rose in my garden. There is a pink form but blue is still the least common colour in gardens and is particularly welcome in spring. Blue comes too with the dwarf bulbous irises. Some are lucky enough to get *Iris reticulata* in February but here it flowers in March. I like the deep purple-blue of the species as much as any of its varieties.

One of my favourite harbingers of spring is *Ipheion uniflorum*, which produces its little pale violet-blue stars from March until May, long after its leaves first appear in the autumn. Formerly called *Tritelia*, its name has been changed by botanists so often it must be dizzy, poor thing. It's easy to grow in a well-drained

13 *Ipheion uniflorum* 'Violaceum'

sunny place, and the few onion-smelling bulbs I begged from my neighbour two years ago have spread quickly.

One sight I wouldn't want to miss in March is the show of the Lent Lilies at Stourhead in Wiltshire. Perhaps this is the best moment to visit this great elysium, but so is the autumn, and it's wonderful too in the snow. Unlike so many of the larger-flowered kinds the wild *Narcissus pseudonarcissus* looks really at home in grass and will spread by seeds if not trampled, picked, or cut down too early. We're a nation of flower-pickers and more's the pity. The Tenby Daffodil, *N. obvallaris*, has a broader trumpet and a stocky habit.

14 The Lent Lilies at Stourhead in spring – a National Trust garden

The earliest large-cupped narcissus in my garden is 'Rijnveld's Early Sensation' which, though short-stemmed and lacking a little in substance, will usually manage February with great ease and January in a sheltered place. Despite its name, 'February Gold' never flowers before March here but we value it and 'Peeping Tom' (a much better name than 'Bartley') for their hardiness and lasting qualities. The swept-back perianth of both derives from *Narcissus cyclamineus*. The species itself naturalises well in moist, peaty soil, producing on four-inch stems its long-trumpeted and sharply reflexed flowers, looking like little golden meteors. 'Tête-à-Tête' is a dwarf early-flowering cultivar with lemon-yellow perianth and orange cup.

Some of the large-flowered trumpet daffodils such as 'Golden Harvest' and 'Dutch Master' will flower outside in March and are excellent for cut flowers. For me they're too large and too highly bred to be ideal for naturalising, and strong foliage, such an asset in other ways, is a nuisance in the border. To grow under shrubs and among ground covers in the border I prefer the dwarf and smaller-flowered kinds such as the *cyclamineus* and *triandrus* hybrids whose foliage soon disappears as the more vigorous perennial plants develop. Most of my early bulbs are set well back in the borders so that the shrubs among which they re planted will also help to screen the aftermath.

Many herbaceous ground-covers too are starting into flower. The Lungworts are a valuable group of shade-loving early flowers of which the familiar spotted-leaved Soldiers and Sailors is one. I grow this, the commonest, for its pink and blue flowers and its white-spotted leaves. For contrast next to it is the form of *Tellima grandiflora* that turns purplish in winter, and a few seedlings of Golden Feverfew. *Pulmonaria saccharata* (or *picta*), especially the form known as 'Margery Fish', has the more sophisticated decoration on its larger leaves but I have a soft spot for the old cottage garden *P. officinalis*. Undoubtedly the showiest in flower are the forms of *P. angustifolia* called 'Azurea', 'Mawson's Variety' and 'Munstead Variety' with plain green hairy leaves and nodding heads of vivid blue flowers.

The first of the bergenias, the pink *B.* × *schmidtii*, is flowering now. You shouldn't forget to cut away some of the evergreen leaves of your epimediums to reveal the delicate little flowers. I like the red and yellow *E.* × *warleyense*. The invaluable hellebores mentioned first by Anne Scott-James in January will go on for a long while yet, both the Lenten Rose and *Helleborus corsicus* whose pale jade bells appear for me by happy accident above a mass of magenta polyanthuses.

Even on alkaline soil we can expect plenty of colour from shrubs this month. Everyone knows the flowering currant and perhaps its less strident but still smelly white form. But I admire particularly the evergreen *Ribes laurifolium* which unfailingly produces its drooping greenish-white flowers against the wall of the gatehouse at Sissinghurst. That superb evergreen *Mahonia japonica* is still flowering and don't despise the Oregon Grape, *Mahonia aquifolium*, an indispensable dwarf shrub with yellow flowers appearing now above leaves burnished by winter winds. Much taller and with prickly sea-green leaves is *M. pinnata* but if

15 The evergreen *Ribes laurifolium* with its drooping greenish flowers

an early-flowering upright evergreen is required, I'd choose 'Undulata' with wavy-edged, lustrous dark green leaves. Pussy Willows are legion, from the tree-like *Salix aegyptica* to the slow-growing *S. hastata* 'Wehrhahnii' with catkins like silver beads on the dark stems.

Cherries are beginning, but in so many areas the flower buds merely provide breakfast for bullfinches, whose sinister beauty is almost equal to that of the graceful March-flowering Yoshino Cherry, *Prunus* × *yedoensis*. But an early flowering tree, called *Alnus sinuata*, is immune to bird damage. Several alders produce elegantly decorative catkins but most are too large and hungry-rooted for the small garden. *Alnus sinuata* is a small tree with conspicuous male catkins up to five or six inches long.

The pace of the gardening year quickens in March and there's so much to be done. Late-flowering shrubs and climbers, like roses, clematises, fuchsias, lavenders, hypericums and plumbagos, need pruning hard; as do dogwoods, purple cotinus, santolinas, and willows grown for their foliage or coloured young stems. Now's the time to give lawns a nitrogenous feed and to apply a balanced compound fertiliser to mixed borders of shrubs and herbaceous plants as well as to roses and soft fruit.

Alas, my sprouting broccoli and November-sown broad beans are dead, but what's left of the spring cabbage and the autumn-sown Japanese onions will need nitrogen to encourage new growth. Soon I shall be picking 'Timperley Early' rhubarb forced under rhubarb pots and I still have carrots, parsnips and leeks from last year's crop. It's safe in March to sow broad beans and of course to plant onion setts and garlic cloves but one must resolve not to be fooled by a false blackthorn spring into sowing other things too early. There is ever something waiting to be done but I enjoy producing vegetables. In fact all gardening is far more fun to do than to write about, to talk about, or even to hear about.

APRIL
by
Peter Coats

April is a very special month for a gardener. Things are really getting going, and the garden is beginning to show some bright colour and some good smells.

When I was a little boy in Scotland, we lived in a large house with a beautiful garden, but like many biggish old houses in Scotland, the garden was nearly a mile and a half from the house. As far away, almost, as the church, to which we dutifully walked for morning service every Sunday. The minister's name was Crawford, and he was a great friend of my family. He had one or two unusual characteristics. First he was a champion tennis player – which impressed me very much – and second, he would occasionally improvise his own prayers, making them up as the fancy struck him. One I always remember, and perhaps it was that which first awoke my interest in plants. This is how it went, in a strong Scottish accent:

> Oh, Lord, who painteth the petal of
> the Polyanthus Purple – shine down
> in all thy power.

Even at that young age polyanthus was one of my favourite flowers – though incidentally, in spite of Mr Crawford's words, I don't think I have ever seen a purple one – they're flowers that come into their own in April, and some of their colours fairly

16 Opposite: Camellias at Nymans, the famous National Trust garden in Sussex

'make the rash gazer wipe his eye' as, I think, Herrick said. There are brilliant yellow polyanthus, crimson polyanthus and a beautiful white and gold one. And now there are bright blue ones, and some that are quite a new, rosy pink. They flower for two months or more, and are really tremendously rewarding.

I wonder how many people know that polyanthus are almost entirely artificial – in fact, they're completely man-made: and made in England too: this happened in the early seventeenth century, and was the result of a cross between the wild cowslip and the primrose – probably *Primula vulgaris* 'Rubra' – the rare pink primrose, which still occasionally occurs in the wild. John Evelyn, who was a good botanist, is the first garden writer to mention the polyanthus by that time, which of course means 'many flowered' from the Greek poly, many, and anthos, a flower. The early varieties of polyanthus raised were usually the mahogany brown, gold-laced or white-laced types. These became favourite florists' flowers, and rivalled the pink and the auricula (of which more later) in the interest and affections of the working men's flower societies in northern England and Scotland. But polyanthus were soon being raised in many other, brighter shades; by the early eighteenth century they were referred to by Robert Thompson in *The Gardener's Assistant* as being 'of unnumbered dyes', and of unnumbered dyes they are, but curiously enough not a real purple.

Polyanthus grow best in half shade, and in soil which has some peat in it to retain moisture. If you have room in your garden to lift them after flowering, and plant them in a cool shady part of the garden, out of the way, they will grow on through the summer, and make large clumps which can be divided and planted out again in autumn. But most gardeners these days can't spare the space, or the time for this particular operation, though it is a good thing to do, if feasible.

Auriculas, which of course are closely related to the polyanthus, are very special flowers indeed. In fact they are, to my mind, some of the most sophisticated plants that exist. Their colours are subtle and understated, and many auriculas, especially the exotic show varieties which really are best grown under glass, have stems and leaves covered with a mealy farina which adds greatly to the plant's charm: these have to be protected from rain, as this would soon spoil the much admired powdery look of the plant.

In the eighteenth century all sorts of extraordinary soil mixtures were recommended for the successful growing of auriculas. Some sound perfectly revolting – however acceptable to the plant. One dedicated auricula grower, Isaac Emmerton, who kept a nursery at Barnet near London, achieved outstanding success, by growing his auriculas in a witches' brew of goose droppings, blood, night soil and 'sugar bakers' scum' – which really confirms the theory that there is no accounting for tastes.

I have said that the colours shown by auriculas are very special, and indeed they seem to flower in colours unknown to any other plant. In the eighteenth century, when their popularity was at its height, it seems that there were auricula flowers in 'slate-blue – a lively green – chamois, cinnamon and moleskin'. And their names were perfectly splendid. 'Black Imperial', 'The Rector of Quatt's Dearest', and 'Mrs Buggs. Her Fine Purple'.

The names of modern auriculas are less striking, but still give an indication of their unique colour range – names such as 'Green Finch', 'Grey Friar' and 'Ginger Bread'.

Auricula seeds can be sown at any time of the year – but the seedlings will seldom come true. That is, perhaps, their fascination. However out of a hundred seedlings there may come one super plant – one that Mrs Buggs herself would be proud of.

April is a great month for flowering trees, and some of the most beautiful of these are magnolias. Beautiful trees, with a beautiful name. They were called after Monsieur Pierre Magnol, a Frenchman who was curator of the Botanical garden at Montpellier in Southern France. Before that, magnolias were called by the cumbrous and unimaginative name of Laurel-Tulip-Tree. I have often thought how lucky it was that Monsieur Magnol was called as he was – supposing he had been called Schmidt 'Come and see our Schmidtias' or 'she has a complexion like a Schmidtia'.

It is curious how almost any name takes on a certain charm if converted into a flower name by the addition of the letter *ia* at the end. Schmidt is an exception, but Smithia would be a perfectly good name for a flower. So would Jonesia – or would it be Joneesia? Try adding *ia* to your own surname and see what happens. I would love to be able to pick a bunch of Coatsias, but I am afraid there is no such plant, nor ever likely to be.

Back to magnolias – one of my great favourites is *Magnolia* × *soulangiana* with its gloriously scented white goblets of flowers, which are sometimes flushed with pink – Soulangiana was also called after a Frenchman, Monsieur Soulange-Bodin, who was director of the Empress Josephine's garden at Malmaison outside Paris. It has an advantage over other magnolias in that it flowers later than most – and thus is less likely to be frosted. Another

17 The narrow petals of *Magnolia stellata*

highly desirable magnolia is *M. stellata* – this flowers in early April, and its flowers have narrow petals and look like stars, hence its name. I was on a garden tour in America some years ago, and I was taken to see a garden near Philadelphia. It was April – but gardens, in the North of America at least, come into flower later than they do in England. There was very little out – except some fine trees of *Magnolia stellata*. It was raining, and I duly admired them, through the window, saying to my hostess, 'How well your stellatas are flowering'. I got a sharp reproof 'Those are not stellatas, Mr Coats, they are Star Magnolias'.

M. kobus is another good magnolia; it comes from Japan, and can grow to a height of thirty feet or so: its great advantage is that, unlike, most magnolias, it will put up with a limey soil. The hybrid *M. × highdownensis* (called after a famous chalk garden) is another magnolia which does not actively mind lime.

Early on in my garden life, I learned a good tip about making magnolias happy. In their wild state, people often forget that magnolias are forest trees and that their natural habitat is woodland. This means that every year they receive a rich mulch of dead leaves, which not only feeds the roots, but keeps them cool. In most European gardens, unless they are woodland gardens like the Royal Horticultural Society garden at Wisley, or very large wild gardens like those at Leonardslea or Nymans, both in Sussex, and open to the public, magnolias are usually grown as specimen trees on a lawn, or on a terrace, or in the hot-dry earth space under the walls of the house. They may do all right, but they'd do far better if mulched at least once a year with dead leaves and compost.

When I was taking photographs in the gardens of Buckingham Palace, for my book, I saw a magnolia which I thought perfectly beautiful, and which I did not know. It was called 'Picture' – and the name suited it very well. It was a form of *M. × soulangiana*, and raised at the famous garden at Exbury in Hampshire, which is better known for azaleas. Picture's flowers are unusual, in that they're held absolutely erect on the branch, and God has really painted their petals purple, or rather splashed them with purple, in a very effective way. The tree I saw in the Palace garden was quite a young one, but from its habit, it did not look as if it would ever grow too big for the average-sized garden of today. So look out for 'Picture'.

Most magnolias smell good, but they do not provide the only good scents of spring. Besides fairly obvious things like narcissus and early lilacs, there are other April scents which I find absolutely intoxicating. That of Balsam Poplar – *Populus balsamifera* – is one. In any garden I have ever had myself – or planned for other people – one of the first trees I have always planted has been a Balsam Poplar. They are not particularly beautiful trees, though they grow quickly, and soon present quite a shapely outline. It is their unfolding spring leaves, which is their great charm. If you touch them, they feel sticky, and their smell – rather like incense – clings to your fingers for hours. And they scent the air for fifty yards around – and further if the wind is in the right direction. I wish whoever it is who chooses the trees to plant along new motorways would sometimes plant Balsam Poplars – I have said that their smell is intoxicating, but it is not as intoxicating as all that – I mean it would not affect drivers, at least I hope not. And it would compete very well with petrol fumes. One important thing, if you want to plant *Populus balsamifera*, ask for it by that name, and *insist* on getting it. A poplar by any other name does *not* smell as sweet. Though some nurseries will tell you that *Populus candicans* does, but they are wrong.

Another shrub which seems to be seldom planted these days, is *Escallonia illinita*. This has a very particular scent – given off by its leaves, rather than by its flowers; it is a scent which may not appeal to everyone, for it is neither exotic, nor particularly spring-like, and it certainly does not remind one of incense. Its leaves emit a strong – but not unpleasing – smell of a farmyard: one might almost say a pigsty. But it is wonderfully rich and earthy, and makes an effective contrast to the more daintily wafted perfumes of Primavera.

Escallonia illinita is evergreen and comes from Chile, and anyone who likes plants which are out of the usual run, and who would like an interesting olfactory experience every April, might find a place for it in their garden . . . up or down wind, according to taste.

Another strongly and more pleasantly scented plant in April is *Osmanthus delavayi*; it has evergreen leaves – dark green and glossy – and white flowers. It's one of the best shrubs for cutting I know, and a few bits of it can scent a whole room. In fact the more you cut the better it grows. Altogether it is a very useful and accommodating thing, and it will grow in almost any soil, if given some shelter from wind: it needs very little pruning. The Royal Horticultural Society Dictionary describes it as one of China's gems, and they are right. It was discovered in Yunnan by that famous plantsman, Abbé Delavay, about eighty years ago. Delavay's name has deservedly been given to several good plants.

A whole family of shrubs which are great favourites of mine are the euphorbias, though scent is hardly their strong point. One, in

18 *Euphorbia wulfenii* – one of the most handsome of euphorbias

fact, and the most handsome of all – *Euphorbia wulfenii* – actually has a rather unpleasant foxy smell, and therefore should not be planted too near the house: but it is a magnificent plant with its bold, architectural outline, and great globular heads of greenish-yellow flowers. There are many euphorbias, all good plants; another which is at its best in spring – earlier than *Euphorbia wulfenii* – is *E. robbiae*. This is a spurge which flowers in April or earlier; it has the greenish-yellow flowers of all spurges, and makes a wonderful flower for cutting, lasting for weeks in water – especially if you burn the stem to seal the 'milk', which, incidentally, can cause irritation if you get it on to your fingers. *Euphorbia robbiae* has another quality: it is one of the few plants which will grow quite happily under yew trees. Euphorbias are said by Pliny to have been named after Euphorbus, who was doctor to the King of Mauritania: so it is possible that the plant was once credited with medicinal powers.

From cabbages to kings – or rather, the other way round. From kings to cabbages. Later in this chapter I must not forget, when dealing with a few rather special annuals, to mention decorative kale, seed of which can be planted this month.

The sarcococcas include several species which are fragrant in early spring. The evergreen *S. confusa, S. hookeriana* and *S. humilis*, all from China, are all deliciously scented, and make attractive shrubs to plant under trees; their fragrance is quite strong in the open air, even in the coldest, dimmest days of spring, and a branch or two brought into the house will scent a room.

Besides Delavay, another French churchman is commemorated by half a dozen plants and trees, Père David. *Viburnum davidii* – that beautiful low growing shrub with bright blue berries – is one, and the Handkerchief Tree – *Davidia involucrata* – is another. The Handkerchief Tree – or, if you are more romantically minded, you can call it the Dove Tree – gets its different pseudonyms from the likeness of its white spring flower bracts to handkerchiefs or doves, whichever you prefer. Actually davidia does not flower until May, so it's jumping the gun a bit to talk about it in April.

Père David not only introduced plants from China, but also, curiously enough, deer. His plants have been very welcome additions to our gardens; his deer (known as Père David's deer – or in Latin, *Elafurus*) should they ever get into any garden, would certainly be less so. They're rather attractive animals to look at, but no respecter of plants, and particularly enjoy eating the bark of newly planted young trees – the rarer the better. They originated in the grounds of the Summer Palace in Peking, and there are some to be seen at Woburn Abbey.

To come down to earth with something of a bump after Chinese palaces and ducal parks – there's some quite important pruning to be done in April. Forsythias, for instance, which have finished flowering, should be pruned in April. I don't terribly like forsythia – I think it is an ugly yellow, and you see such an awful lot of it. If I were planting a new garden, and had room, I should try to treat it as a crop. I should plant it as a hedge, or windbreak, in the kitchen garden, and cut it right down as soon as it had had some frost on it, and its flower buds were showing. These branches I would bring into the house, and put in a pail of water in a warm room. They soon come out, and look very bright and cheerful as decoration – and they last well. 'Lynwood' is a good variety of forsythia, and is not quite such a strident yellow as the other types.

Another shrub which can be treated like this is the ordinary flowering currant or ribes – and an added advantage of treating ribes like this, is that the flowers, when forced, are pale pearly white, and not the acid pink that they are in nature.

To go back to forsythia for a moment – it might be of interest to mention that it was named after William Forsyth, who was King George III's Scottish gardener at Kensington. There is a statue of him, placed in a grove of forsythias, in Hyde Park.

Other shrubs which can be pruned in April are the early flowering spiraeas, and chaenomeles, otherwise *Pyrus japonica*, otherwise cydonia. No unfortunate plant has had its name changed so often as the unfortunate quinces – no wonder they are sour.

One variety of chaenomeles (I think that is the currently correct name) that I particularly like is the seldom grown, 'Moerloosii' which has lovely clusters of pink and white flowers. It's best grown on a wall, and can grow as tall as nine foot in a very few years.

Lavender can be lightly clipped in April, to prevent the bushes becoming out of shape. In fact, lavender is one of the shrubby plants which can be really cut hard back, and usually be relied on to 'come again', though it may protest by not flowering over-generously the same year.

Last summer, in a friend's garden in Oxfordshire, I saw a lavender hedge planted in what I thought was a very attractive and original way – it was composed of mauve and pink lavender bushes set alternately: and I wonder how many people know that there is a delightful white flowered lavender – *Lavandula spica* 'Alba' – slightly less strongly scented than the other type, but full of charm. It is said to have been the favourite flower of the unfortunate Queen Henrietta Maria. In the inventory of the auction of her possessions at her Manor at Wimbledon, under the Commonwealth, 'very great and large borders of white lavender' were among the items for sale.

Another little known lavender is *Lavandula stoechas*, with strongly aromatic, slightly sticky, leaves. It is a native of the Mediterranean islands of the Stoechades, or Iles de Hyères – and its endearing old English name is Stickadove.

No notes on the garden in April could be complete without mention of camellias – though in any reasonable year these should have been flowering since February. Camellias are surely one of the most beautiful – and most romantic, of shrubs. They got their mellifluous name from a simple Jesuit priest, Georg Kamel, who was sent to the Philippines and China as a missionary in the late seventeenth century, and sent back seeds of the plants he found there. Thirty years after he died – in 1704 – his work for botany was recognised, and his name was given to a beautiful race of plants, seeds of which he may (it is not known) or may not have, introduced to the Western World. The K of his name was changed to C (there being no K in the Latin alphabet) and so the beautiful plant name – *Camellia* – came into being.

It is curious how almost everyone mispronounces the camellia's name. 'The French get it right' I wrote, once, years ago 'but Anglo-Saxons persist in pronouncing the second syllable to rhyme with "feel" instead of "fell" – which is illogical and incorrect.'

Some camellias I particularly like are all the *sasanqua* group with their delicately sculptured flowers – which somehow look more natural than those of most camellias; the triumphantly artificial looking 'Countess Lavinia Maggi', which has white flowers striped in carmine, and the deep red 'Ville de Nantes', which always appears to flower for a longer period than any other camellia. But it is impossible to pick out one's favourite camellias. They are all so beautiful. No wonder Dumas' consumptive heroine, Marguerite Gautier, loved them: though the unromantic reason she gave was that, as camellias have no scent, they were the only flowers that did not make her sneeze.

April is the time for sowing annuals. Nowadays not many people seem to have the time for these, and I think it's a great pity. Annuals are wonderfully useful for brightening up the garden in August and September, when the exuberance and colour of the herbaceous border – or shrub border for that matter – are just a little past their best.

Besides the obvious annuals – like petunias, antirrhinums and nicotianas, there are three which I would warmly recommend. The first is *Echium* 'Blue Bedder', which can be sown where you want it to flower and thinned out – the more ruthlessly the better, soon after it has made young seedlings. *Echium* starts flowering at the end of June, and goes on till the first frosts. It makes a haze of blue flowers, and the leaves are a silvery green.

The second annual I particularly like is *Cleome spinosa* – one of the Spider Flowers, from the spidery form of its petals. This is a plant which has to be started under glass, and only planted out when all danger of frost is passed – but it is a beautiful thing, and always attracts attention. It needs a warm position, a light soil and lots of room. It is well worth a try, and most good firms can supply seed.

The third in my list of special annual plants which can be sown this month – under glass preferably – is the decorative or ornamental cabbage, or kale. This is a gloriously colourful form of cabbage – *Brassica oleracea* – which can be planted out in June. For the rest of the summer, and well into the winter, if the weather is not too hard, it will present spectacular bouquets of multicoloured leaves which greatly add to the gaiety of the herbaceous border. The secret of achieving a good display is to plant the seedlings eight or ten inches apart, to make a solid splash of colour. Planted

19 The glorious ornamental cabbage with curled leaves

further apart, as you would usually set brassicas, decorative kale or cabbage plants are less effective.

I have almost finished these notes on the garden in April, and suddenly realise that I have hardly mentioned tulips – which are really the star performers in gardens in April and May. I came across a quotation the other day about tulips – which, if not very technical or instructive, made me smile. I found it in one of the best of all garden books *Les Fleurs Animées* – a book published in France in the forties of the last century, and beautifully illustrated by Albert Grandville.

As is well known, the Dutch, usually rather staid and sensible, went completely off their heads about tulips during the time of the

20 A cabbage with a heart of pink

21 The elegant lily-flowered tulip, 'Ellen Willmott'

Tulpenwoede or Tulipomania, of the sixteenth century – and they gambled on tulip bulbs like people do on horses today. A farmyard full of animals would be exchanged for one bulb. Some years later, an article making fun of the Dutch, and their obsession with tulips, appeared in the *Tatler*, soon after Richard Steele started that magazine in 1709. It records an overheard conversation:

As I sat in the porch, I heard the voices of two or three persons, who seemed very earnest in discourse. My curiosity was raised when I heard the names of Alexander the Great and Artaxerxes; and as their talk seemed to run on ancient heroes, I concluded there could not be any secret in it; for which reason I thought I might fairly listen to what they said.

After several parallels between great men, which appeared to me altogether groundless and chimerical, I was surprised to hear one say, that he valued the Black Prince more than Duke of Vendôme. How the Duke of Vendôme should become a rival of the Black Prince, I could not conceive; and was more startled when I heard a second affirm, with great vehemence, that if the Emperor of Germany was not going off, he should like him better than either of them. He added, that though the season was so changeable, the Duke of Marlborough was in blooming beauty. I was wondering to myself from whence they had received this odd intelligence: especially when I heard them mention the names of several other generals such as the Prince of Hesse and the King of Sweden, who, they said, were apt to run away. But they added, that the Marshall Villars kept his colours well.

At last, one of them told the company, that if they would go along with him, he would show them something which would please them very much. A Chimney-Sweeper and a Painted Lady in the same bed.

Two Dutch Tulipomaniacs talking about their favourite flower.

22 Great Dixter – a view of the topiary

MAY

by

Christopher Lloyd

May is not a peak month in most gardens, and mine is no exception in this regard. Only the woodland gardens, dominated by their rhododendrons and azaleas, reach their climax now. And they suffer for it later in the caterpillar-ridden gloom of high summer: unrelieved, apart from token plantings of hostas and hydrangeas, until the next rhododendron season comes around.

May is the month that all romantic poets and novelists have celebrated as epitomising youth and young love. This image is created by nature itself. The whole countryside is a garden. Attempts by gardeners to improve on nature in May are futile. Rhododendron gardeners themselves often succeed in ruining the setting with a cacophony of brilliant and jarring colour juxtapositions. Is this an improvement on a bluebell wood, or a carpet of anemones and primroses? I doubt it.

When the countryside turns dark and heavy in July, then the gardener's art comes truly into its own. That art, of keeping the garden fresh and gay right into autumn – and it's a craft as well as an art – becomes ever more testing as the season advances. Autumn being my favourite season, I enjoy all that. But here we are in May, when the foundations are laid.

Great Dixter, where I live in East Sussex, is a garden of firm outlines, designed by Lutyens and by my father, mostly just before the First World War. Yew and box hedges and topiary, walls and old farm buildings, form its bones; but the planting is, and always has been, informal.

There are many borders and they are all of a mixed nature, including shrubs, hardy and tender plants, annuals, bulbs – anything that seems to fit in and make a living tapestry. The Long Border is typical. It is seventy yards long, fifteen feet wide, and backed by a yew hedge; and a flagstone path runs along the front. The border is by no means full yet, but the bare earth is no disgrace until the height of its season is reached. Foliage is playing a dominant role: the spears of irises contrasting with broader leaves such as the cardoon's – grey, deeply cut, lush, growing at a great pace. They're already four feet long.

23 Mixed planting in the Long Border

Some shrubs, grown just for their leaves, are looking their best: for instance, a well-known evergreen member of the spindle family, *Euonymus fortunei* 'Silver Queen'. Normally its leaf is green in the centre with a white margin, but young leaves are bright butter-yellow at their margins, so there is a marked contrast in the young foliage seen against the old.

Then there is the golden cut-leaved elder, *Sambucus racemosa* 'Plumosa Aurea'. In this the lacy, heavily fringed leaf is copper as it first appears in April, changing to bright yellow soon, and then gradually through lime to pale green in late summer. Flowers would detract from the foliage effect, and I prevent them being produced by cutting the shrub hard back each winter.

Colour from flowers is gradually being added in, but I always have to bear in mind that the border's main season is from late June till September. Nothing must detract from this by flowering, finishing, and leaving a nasty dull spot prematurely. So now there are forget-me-nots that sow themselves harmlessly among border perennials, and dog-violets nestled under deciduous shrubs which will later cast too dense a shade for anything else to grow so near them. There's a carpet of woodruff under an escallonia – brilliant green foliage surmounted by heads of tiny, purest white, cruciform flowers. And I'm rather proud of a colony of toothwort, *Lathraea clandestina*, that I've lately established at the foot of a silver willow, from a lump of roots given me by a friend.

The hooded flowers are clustered close to ground level and they are brilliant purple – almost an aniline dye – rather like crocuses at their first appearance in March, but flowering on untiringly till the end of May. That's all you can see of the plant. It's a complete parasite, never producing its own leaves, but feeding off the roots of its host, generally willow or poplar. Planting a parasite is an unfamiliar ploy to me, so I just interred it close to the willow's trunk and hoped that it would get the idea. And it did.

I particularly love tulips and the gladdening way their blooms open in response to warmth and sunlight. They can be worked in among perennials that need only occasional disturbance; and the tulips themselves, which love a heavy soil like mine, go on for many years without being lifted or harvested or in any way fussed over.

Oriental poppies start flowering in the second half of the month, and I include three colours: the typical scarlet kind (I remember how Vita Sackville-West shuddered at the vulgarity of its raucous colouring, but I get a great thrill from it seen in this foliage setting, as the Long Border still is); then there is the salmon-pink 'Mrs Perry'; and the dark crimson-red 'Goliath' – an upstanding plant that seldom needs support. When oriental poppies have flowered they look a mess, but they have the great merit of not in the least resenting being cut to the ground at this stage. Neighbouring plants like Japanese anemones and perennial asters will soon fill the gap. In 'Goliath's' case, I resort to another device. The plants are cut down and lifted, after flowering, and lined out in a spare row, being returned to their flowering positions in late autumn. Meantime I can plant this vacated site with some fast-growing annual like tithonias (which are like giant zinnias) or with cannas for foliage effect.

Lupins flower at the same time, from late May into June, but can't be treated in the same way. They look derelict after flowering, whatever you do to them. But for colour and scent, and for the proud way they bear themselves, and the way bees crowd around them, they are much too much fun to be left out. So I grow them in two large patches in another part of the garden. One patch is interplanted with tulips, which flower two or three weeks earlier; the other with a blue Dutch iris – one of the bulbous kinds. That's an experiment, and I am not sure yet how it will work out. Irises and lupins should flower simultaneously.

After that I shall harvest the bulbs, throw the lupins away, and plant up with annuals – cosmeas, mallows, and cleomes (the spider flowers). Meantime I've sown more lupins for next year's display, and I'm treating them as biennials, not as perennials at all.

There is another kind of perennial in the Long Border that pays its rent over and over again, either by flowering continuously,

24 The salmon–pink poppy *Papaver orientale* 'Mrs Perry'

25 One of the Long Border's most useful perennials, *Viola cornuta* 'Alba'

without encouragement, the season through, or by being made to start afresh, half-way through its season, and doing its stuff all over again. *Viola cornuta* 'Alba' comes usually into the second category. It has a pure white pixie-like flower, and leaves of a particularly fresh green, as is often the way with albino plant forms. All of us have to garden *with* our soil, rather than fight against its natural properties, and here at Dixter we overlie Wadhurst clay, a heavy, water-retentive soil which is just what the viola relishes. It is opening its first blooms now, and if the spring, summer and autumn remain drenching wet throughout, it will flower non-stop, untiringly, for a six-month stretch. If, as is more likely (and as perhaps some of us hope), the weather turns hot and dry at some stage, or if it is attacked by greenfly in June, the viola will falter. I shall slash it all to ground level with a large knife, dose it with a compound fertiliser, give it a thorough soaking, and away it will go as though spring had only just arrived. It is the same with the giant chives, which are just as tasty as ordinary chives, but, additionally, a thoroughly showy plant in flower, with globular, rather scabious-like heads in various shades of rosy mauve. Its first flush comes in May. Then, out with the knife, and within a week the plants are refurnished with delicious young foliage, and they will flower a second, sometimes even a third, time.

Some of the cranesbills are terrific stayers. These are the true geraniums and nearly all of them are hardy plants. I have half a dozen different kinds in the Long Border, and they will all be flowering this month. One of my favourites is called 'Russell Prichard'. It is a mat-forming plant: a large loose mat, perhaps a pool rather than a mat, as it flows forwards on to the path and reaches back into other plants taller than itself, threading its way among their stems, and reappearing at quite unexpected heights. This is a typically endearing cranesbill trick, and invaluable for binding a border's ingredients together, so that there is no frontier between one group of plants and the next. 'Russell Prichard's' flowers are brilliant magenta. Some of my friends find all magentas repulsive, and they can be weak and muddy with too much blue in them, but a strong, clear magenta is something to wallow and revel in: particularly striking, actually, when seen in rough meadow grass in a background that is predominantly lush green. There are clumps of an early-flowering very prolific gladiolus species in the Long Border, *Gladiolus byzantinus*. This is magenta, and looks well in its border setting for a fortnight or so, at the turn of this month and next, but I have transferred it to rough grass at various times, and it adapts splendidly to these tougher conditions, and makes a surprising contrast to the strong yellow of buttercups. But all is leavened by the grasses themselves. You never feel 'this is too much'.

Rough grass plays a very important and rather unorthodox part in the gardens at Dixter, and turns up in various unexpected places, so that some tidy-minded visitors are given to think we're desperately short of labour and have had to abandon certain areas. But in fact it gives rise to a style of gardening in its own right, one that my mother was especially fond of and initiated at Dixter from the very start, when we had nine gardeners as against three now. It is a fact that if a meadow is left wholly untouched by fertilisers or any kind of manure, its tapestry and wealth of flower varieties will be of the richest. And so, when the gardens were laid out here nearly seventy years ago, certain pieces of grass turf were simply left. Others, as where a moat was drained, were created. Their only treatment is by cutting, twice or three times a year, in July, in August, and again in November. In this way, the grasses are prevented from becoming coarse and tussocky.

And so, on the other side of the paved walk that flanks the Long Border, is first a strip of mown grass, and then a daffodil orchard. Just now, of course, the daffodils are going over, but their 'flopping masses of decay', as Reginald Farrer described their ageing foliage, are concealed by the lengthening grasses, and, in all the moist, shadier spots, by a grand display of cow parsley. 'You *do* grow parsley here,' one visitor remarked – morosely, I thought. I could only say, 'We like it', and he grunted, ferociously.

Presently, in all the sunniest areas there will be a huge carpet of moon daisies. In the morning they all look east towards the Long Border, but by the afternoon they've turned their backs on it, and you must walk to the bottom of the orchard, turn round, and admire them with the Long Border as a distant prospect.

The natural meadow flora is plentiful but we have added a great deal to it, always in the hope that whatever we've given a start will take so happily to its new surroundings that it will increase, generally by self-sowing, and thus carry on with the good work by itself. In this way we have been particularly successful in naturalising a number of native orchid species. The early purples, *Orchis mascula*, are flowering just now, soon to be followed by the green-winged *Orchis morio*, and that by the spotted orchis. *Dactylorhiza fuchsii* it's called now, but we knew it better as *Orchis maculata*. This has really run riot, seeding itself not only in the turf but in the borders and in paving cracks.

In my unregenerate youth, before we understood about conservation, my mother and I used to sally forth into the neighbour-

26 A British native orchid, *Dactylorhiza fuchsii* better known as *Orchis maculata*, part of the natural meadow flora at Great Dixter

ing woods, and fields, carrying a large trug-basket between us, and armed with long, strong fern-trowels. The green-winged orchis grew in certain old undisturbed pastures but, once the style of farming altered and all grassland was visited from time to time by the plough, this orchis was wiped out; and I cannot but rejoice at the way it has adopted us so enthusiastically at Dixter, even seeding itself in the thin turf that covers the reservoir at the top of our garden. Next to the front path leading to the house there is a colony of some one hundred and fifty spikes in most years.

Perhaps the most relaxing spot in the whole garden – at least I find it so and often lie on the turf near its side – is the horse-pond. It's a 'natural' pond, with a muddy clay bottom, and at one time the farm-horses were led into it to drink. But centuries earlier, this was all part of iron-ore workings, of which there are such numerous traces in the Weald of Kent and Sussex. Still water and its reflections have a fascination for all of us but it never remains still for very long. The surface is constantly being broken. One gets a strong sense of a living community in and around a pond. Swallows are back, skimming and dipping over the water. Various birds make a habit of drinking from the water-lily pads, notably goldfinches, linnets, and pied wagtails. Moorhens will be nesting presently. There is not enough cover for them yet, but they're around a lot, and will rear their second brood here. Dragonflies of many sizes and colours are hatching, and there are grass snakes, which would be much more appropriately termed water snakes. I haven't seen one yet, but others have. They come out and bask on the dead old gunnera leaves. *Gunnera manicata* is a dramatic bankside plant. In winter there's nothing to be seen but humpy rhizomes and heaps of dead foliage. It looks as if someone had been dredging the pond. But now its young leaves are expanding, and presently they will be six feet tall and five across: huge, undulating umbrellas with spiny stems. Just as prominent at this moment are its extraordinary flower spikes, shaped like some primeval fir-cone or fertility symbol. Gunneras hail from the highlands of Brazil. They are the largest-leaved hardy plants that we can grow in Britain, and they are splendid ground-coverers and weed-suppressors.

The water saxifrage, *Peltiphyllum peltatum*, is a kind of mini-gunnera, with a similar umbrella leaf, but only two or three feet tall. It is equally efficient ground-cover on a pond bank, and it is flowering now, before any leaf has unfurled. Fleshy stems, not unlike a rhubarb stalk but hairy, are crowned by a bonnet of delightful pink starry blossoms.

Self-sown wild brooms also favour the lip of the pond bank,

and another good wild plant is the poisonous water dropwort, *Oenanthe crocata*. It has umbels of white blossom like cow parsley, but is a far bolder, more effective plant, and looks especially good with the yellow flag irises, which will grow both on the bank and under water. Members of the arum family, including the white florist's arum, are often fond of water, and will grow inches below the surface. A May-flowerer among these is *Orontium aquaticum*, the golden club, which produces a large cluster of serpentine flowering stems which are yellow at their tips and white behind them.

Of the vegetable garden I should, I realise, be able to say that broad beans sown last autumn are already flowering and alive with bees; that the peas will not be slow in following and have their supporting sticks in position; that brassicas are being lined out from their seed beds, that we're pulling early carrots and so on and so forth.

But it isn't like that at all at Dixter. I'm crazy about vegetables and there are few I don't relish, but flowers come first and there are too many tasks in their respect each spring for the vegetables to get a look-in until very late.

We haven't even planted our potatoes yet. I grow the extraordinary 'Pink Fir Apple', which looks more like a warty Jerusalem artichoke than a potato. It is waxy and yellow, when cooked, no use for baking or mashing but it never boils to a mush and it really does have a delicious flavour eaten hot, or cold in a salad. That's my opinion, anyway, but I should perhaps warn that some potato gluttons, unless particularly well-mannered, would leave it on the side of their plate.

Peas and broad beans will be sown at the end of the month. We're usually eating – and freezing them, for no two home-grown vegetables lend themselves better to this purpose – in August and September. They'll be no less welcome for being late and there is this great advantage, seeing that our soil lies wet and cold till late into most springs: the seeds won't rot in the ground and they won't need to be dressed against rotting.

I did sow calabrese in a pot last month and the seedlings are just ready for potting off individually prior to being planted out in June. Expensive F_1 hybrid seed that is liable to disappear if committed direct to the open ground, deserves this princely treatment and I shall repeat it next month for the late-developing 'Late Corona' calabrese, which will take over in September and continue cropping for as long as the winter remains open – right on till April, if the year is specially favourable.

I know this green-sprouting broccoli is a great favourite with the commercial deep-frozen vegetable producers and I freeze it myself in times of glut but the fact has to be admitted that most of its flavour disappears in the processing so the longer you can be picking it fresh, the happier the outcome. Boil it in plenty of water, so as to retain the colour; never for longer than ten minutes and eat it straightaway. If kept hot and made to wait it becomes as discoloured and distasteful as sprouts treated in the same way.

We have a large globe artichoke bed, this being one of our favourite vegetables and there is a lot to be said for replanting half your stock in early May every year, if you can get around to it. Old plants crop in June and July and then finish. But if you take rooted offsets now, just one crown to each unit, shortening the leaves by half to reduce transpiration and lining them out three feet apart – yes, artichokes are extravagant of space but there is no handsomer crop – then, given the water they'll need in times of drought, they'll crop from August till the end of October, carrying the largest heads of the highest quality. In all, then, you'll be enjoying artichokes for a five month stretch. And if you really love them you can never be surfeited.

It's the same with figs and my last word shall be to fellow fig-lovers. Figs were planted on the walls at Dixter for the bold and handsome patterns created by their foliage. The variety used was 'Brunswick', whose leaf has the deepest recesses. Fortunately this fig also carries, in its good years, large and luscious fruits. They are borne near the ends of last year's shoots, so the less pruning you can get away with, the better.

Now is the time to examine these shoots and obtain a clue to what the fig prospects are. The young fruits are just about the size of a pea, but they will rapidly swell, and one must then hope that the majority will be retained through the danger period in late June when many are liable to drop off.

JUNE
by
Hugh Johnson

I wonder if I'm the only gardener who relishes a rainy spring. In Essex the spring sensation of lush growth is usually tempered (bad-tempered, that is) by drying winds straight from what we call the East Pole. Getting new trees and shrubs established is a frustrating business. But in a rainy year even the County Council's tree-planting – they always put them in far too big – can get away to a flying start.

Admittedly I'm more concerned with new plantations than most people, being a newish gardener, and in a flat part of England where your average field is about a hundred acres and all the elms are dead or dying. Replacing shelter from the gales that can come from any corner has been my biggest problem since I came here eight years ago.

The name of our village is Saling, which is supposed to come from the same ancient root as the Anglo-Saxon sallow and also the Latin salix – an open invitation to grow willows which I have gladly accepted. They like our heavy soil; they are, in the main, a hardy and vigorous race, and there seems no end to their variations on a theme: they must be the most varied family in the whole botany book.

But nobody bothers about willows in June – there are far more glamorous things about. I came across a mysterious reference in a modern manual recently to 'the June gap'. I've heard of July gaps and August gaps, but what is there a gap in, in June? The Chelsea

Show is not at the end of May by chance. As the rhododendrons pass their peak the roses start up; laburnum and lilac follow the cherries; and the best and most popular of all the border plants – irises, lupins, poppies, peonies – do their stuff. It is the month of lilies, there are strawberries to pick, and salads have their big moment.

The greatest change of all that has come over the garden since a month ago is that it has gone solid. The transparency and sketchiness of winter and spring have gone. The bare earth has gone, or almost. And, above all, you can't see through trees and bushes any more. The voids in the tracery have filled up, giving each part of the garden the shape you always imagine it to have, with the other bits blocked out.

I get such satisfaction from this simple fact – the sense of enclosure, privacy, calm, that the green walls of June produce – that I am slowly converting more and more of the dividers of my garden to evergreen. Solidity in winter is even more valuable than in summer. It is odd how light and warmth seem to have somehow got out of kilter. Here we are wondering if we can finally put our bedsocks away, and the longest day is coming up in less than three weeks. To me the length of the days is the special magic of June – the light after dinner and long before breakfast. I find it hard to drag myself in from the garden as late as half past ten at night. And of course the further north you go the more climactic June is. We spent a family holiday in fairly northern Sweden, at mid-summer, two or three years ago, and returned completely whacked, hardly having gone to bed at all, so lovely were the nights that never really got dark.

There are two things about June nights, or rather the early mornings or late evenings, that make them, along with days of misty sunlight in October and perhaps the brilliant days of hoar frost in mid-winter, the most beautiful of all in the garden. One is the air, cool and soft and pregnant with scents of growth and flowering, and the other is the light, at a level and quality that gives the paler colours their utmost luminosity, and deepens the dark ones into velvet pools. I always think it is a pity that the great show gardens are never open early and late. You have to go about eleven in the morning, and you're turned out about tea-time. Seeing them only round the middle of the day with the sun at its height we never see them at their best at all.

For most gardeners, I should think, certainly for me, June is before everything the time of roses. Having rather a big garden I am not myself desperate that everything should be perpetual-flowering. In certain key places it is certainly an advantage, but on the whole I'm very happy with roses that flower once, marvellously, then perhaps sporadically with a few wistful reminders in the autumn. I realise that in a small garden such an attitude is impractical. But the once-for-all sweetness of certain flowers is an important ingredient of garden pleasure – and we don't expect tulips to come popping up again in August.

The roses that are coming up now to do their incomparable acts and then retire are the old gallicas and damasks and albas, the Scotch roses, the wonderful English dog rose, of course, and the exotic dog roses which are the pure wild species of all sorts of places from Virginia to the Himalayas; and, most spectacularly of all, the mighty climbers of the musk group, on a scale that eats a small tree for breakfast and is in the top of an oak by lunchtime. *Rosa filipes* 'Kiftsgate', called after the next-door garden to Hidcote in the Cotswolds, has a reputation for being the biggest of the lot, but there is little to choose between several of them for vigour.

I am particularly fond of 'Wedding Day', which has filled a substantial pear tree in four years at Saling. Its buds are warm yellow, in trusses sometimes three or four feet long. When the flowers open, they are creamy-white with a marvellous smell of oranges which carries for miles. Later, especially after rain, they develop pink speckles which put some people off, I'm told, but which I find yet another attraction.

I also have in the garden a little-known climber of almost frightening vigour, with the lovely name of 'Mrs Honey Dyson'. She has rather round double flowers of a peachy complexion and

28 *Rosa filipes* 'Kiftsgate', a vigorous climber

sweet breath and her leaves have a pale greyish cast. In the garden at Chipping Sodbury where I got her she had been too much altogether for an old apple tree and borne it to the ground. Unfortunately though she is one of those roses which hang onto their petals after fading. The exquisite alba, 'Great Maiden's Blush', I find does the same, ending up covered in tatty brown balls. I never have time to deadhead anything so this is a serious disadvantage.

My choice for the single most useful rose is paradoxically the one with the dowdiest flowers – the little pink *Rosa rubrifolia* – a dog rose to take to the bosom of your garden, where with a bit of luck it will seed in places you wouldn't imagine possible.

29 A close-up of Rose 'Wedding Day'

Why should you want dowdy dog-rose seedlings in unlikely places? Because *rubrifolia* has leaves of a colour, and deportment of a character, that put it in my list of the ten best plants. The leaves combine a tender grey-blue with a light reddy-purple to produce a smoky effect that sets off almost any colour in the garden; and the slender red stems, with hardly any thorns, arch into a graceful unaggressive bush, perhaps six or seven feet high, which seems to take up hardly any space and certainly casts hardly any shade. The best moment of this paragon is in September, when the flowers you scarcely noticed suddenly reveal their purpose: slender little hips of orangey brown which go wonderfully well with the bluey leaves. It is worth sowing a row of these hips for plants for your friends. Your own new plants will soon announce themselves as unmistakable pinky-blue seedlings in beds, walls, and crannies – each one a brainwave.

The early roses which I specially love but don't very often see in gardens are the Scotch briars. I think I am right in using the name for a whole group of varying sizes with masses of prickles and bristles too (whence their Linnaean name of *Rosa spinosissima* – now alas changed to *R. pimpinellifolia*). There are some exquisitely dainty little bushes among them, with masses of tiny fretted leaves of pale sea-green, and double (sometimes single but usually double) completely unsophisticated little flowers whose scent Graham Thomas describes as 'penetrating and delicious, as fresh as lily of the valley'. I'll have to quote Graham Thomas on their autumn performance, too, as it gives an extra reason for growing them to people who spurn once-flowering roses. Their 'dark fruits often add to a remarkable display of sombre leaf colour; grey-brown and plum vie with maroon and dark red in intensity, with an orange or yellow leaf here and there'.

I grow the 'Double White' and the brilliant little single crimson called 'William III'. Regent's Park used it on their stand at Chelsea the year they had a ruined mill and a sunken dinghy. It grew by the water wheel and people queued up to read its label. The Dunwich rose from the sand dunes of the Suffolk coast is a single white one; and the glorious great yellow 'Frühlingsgold' is half Scotch briar and half hybrid tea.

The loveliest bush of the tribe I have ever seen was one called 'Glory of Edzell', at Crathes Castle near Aberdeen. It stooped under the combined weight of its deep pink flowers and a sparkling shower of rain. But, come to think of it, that must have been in May, because the lovely yellow *Paeonia mlokosewitschii* was out too, among a host of pale pink bluebells. They are very early roses.

We have no rhododendrons. For some reason I find them very difficult plants to love – which is just as well, since chalky boulder clay and nineteen inches of rain a year virtually rules them out. If something splendidly scarlet and twenty feet high catches your

30 Rose 'Frühlingsgold', a glorious yellow

eye in a glade at Saling in June, it is nothing more exotic than a hawthorn – but a good hawthorn, red or white, is not to be scorned. 'Paul's Scarlet' is the best. One singular virtue of haw- thorns is that their pretty pale leaves come out so early in the spring.

The really posh plants favoured by the grand gardeners tend to be the ones with fleshy or waxy flowers: the stately magnolias, camellias, and the like with petals of real substance – the very opposite of the papery petals of such ephemeral plants as cistuses and mallows. One tends to associate – at least I tend to associate – big open flimsy flowers with hot dry places – probably for no good reason. That is why I was amazed to discover that the magnificent tree mallow, *Abutilon vitifolium*, grows wild in southern Chile with a rainfall higher than Argyll – something of the order of two hundred inches a year. No plant I know makes such a show so quickly. Planted on a south wall it reached twenty feet (which is twice the height of the wall) in three years in my garden, and in the second and third years was covered for weeks with its wide open flowers of palest mauve, opening from soft olive-furry buds. The extremely handsome vine-shaped leaves, also pale grey-olive, are evergreen, too, most of them – at least they are here.

More by luck than judgement, like most of the best things in my garden, its neighbours in flower are *Ceanothus dentatus*, an evergreen ceanothus of a lovely pale pure blue (and another express grower), and the noble great Goat's beard *Aruncus sylvester* (or *A. dioicus* as the botanists now call it), which puts up buff- coloured plumes from a tall fern-like foundation. Aruncus sets off everything to perfection – old roses particularly. Really blue flowers are always rare. But for June, to flower with the prettiest, most fragrant, and one of the earliest of the day lilies, the pale yellow *Hemerocallis flava* – there is a splendid rich blue boragey plant called *Anchusa* 'Loddon Royalist'. This is one of those plants which knocks you out in its first year, is half-good the second and no good at all the third. You must take root cuttings and start again – or go back to the nursery and buy more.

In the end I settled for the less true-blue but utterly reliable and permanent cranesbill, *Geranium ibericum*, which, as its clumps spread, gets hacked up and carried to the wilder ends of the garden where its weed-smothering capabilities will be tested to the limit. They haven't failed me yet.

I am not, to be honest, a great lupin-lover. I've tried a number with fancy names and found fault with them all. The worst was one called 'Thundercloud', whose purple flowers turned a sorry brown and stayed put. I don't mind the muddled pink of wayward seedlings (though I should much prefer the violet-blue lupin of the wild west) but the lupin we should all grow is the oddly-named tree lupin, which in reality is a sprawling bush with masses of sweet-scented creamy white or yellow flowers. It doesn't live long, but it seeds itself.

You could make a marvellous garden with plants that sow themselves, simply by weeding out what you didn't want. There are plenty of annuals, and biennials of course, that come round again automatically like love-in-a-mist, opium poppies, honesty, mulleins, foxgloves, the giant thistle, and *Eryngium giganteum*, which is known as Miss Willmott's ghost. *Rosa rubrifolia* I have mentioned, and tree lupins, and hebes, and hellebores. It is certainly the first rule of weeding never to pull up what you can't identify. A very useful tip, by the way, and again from Graham Thomas, is that you can tell if foxgloves are going to be mauve or white as soon as you find the seedlings. The mauve ones have a purply flush in their leaf-stalks from birth. The white, of course, are some of the loveliest wildlings in the world.

For sheer spectacle and bravado, to give a real bit of punch to a border in June, there is nothing quite so effective as the eremuruses or foxtail lilies. Their great green proboses push up so early in the year that you expect the worst from frost. But mine have never suffered, just built up fountains of broad strap-leaves until the spike is ready to go. Then up it goes to seven or eight feet, crowned with a column of hundreds of little lilies. *E. robustus* is light pink, and *E. himalaicus* white (and earlier). They are re-

31 The grand spikes of *Eremurus robustus*

markably gale-proof, permanent and undemanding – yet nobody can deny they are grand.

Another spike-flowering plant which could not be less trouble, yet one very rarely sees, is *Asphodeline lutea*, the yellow asphodel. Its grassy grey leaves in a curious formation are evergreen, which is always a virtue in herbaceous plants, helping in a small way to make the garden look alive in winter. The spikes are perhaps a yard high, and the flowers jut out around, shining bright. Later come green marble-like seeds. It may not make the First Eleven as a patch of riotous colour but every visitor stops and asks what it is, which is not a bad test.

There are more seductive scents in the garden in June than at any other time. Philadelphus, lilac, hawthorn, brooms, honeysuckle, roses and pinks are all impregnating the air, and at the end of the month the lime tree, with the most swooningly sweet breath of all, joins in. There are two indispensable smells which, ideally, you should persuade your neighbours to provide, since the plants that make them are not quite worth your precious space. Philadelaphus is one: the ugliest bush, however pure and perfumed its flowers. Sweetbriar is the other: not a particularly good-looking rose and fiendishly prickly, but sending out an achingly beautiful smell of apples mysteriously generated in its leaves. A hedge of sweetbriar and honeysuckle to windward conjures up Puck and Titania and Bottom the weaver.

The way botanists keep changing names is the keen gardener's second favourite complaint, after the weather. I had always thought, from the way philadelphus is still almost universally called syringa by the laity, that its name-change must have been within living memory at least. Not a bit of it. It was Linnaeus, two hundred years ago, who changed it. Before that syringa was also known as pipe-tree – for what is a syringe but a pipe in Greek? Of course, syringa brings confusion since this is the Latin name for lilac. Did you know, by the way, that philadelphus leaves taste of cucumber?

Ah yes, salads. The inner man can comfort himself, as the asparagus departs, with the approach of the broad bean. Broad beans should never be allowed to grow bigger than peas. Then they should be just blanched and eaten cold as a salad. I think the best salad I ever had was made like this with the tiny broad beans and leaves of salad rocket, which the Italians call *ruccheta* and no one else seems to bother with. Rocket is a savoury, rich-tasting slightly peppery herb, and with the two we put purslane, which the French call *Pourpier doré*, a sprawling little green with succulent leaves and stems – not much taste but a clean crisp bite. The beans, purslane, and rocket, with oil and salt and hardly any vinegar, had the taste of the June garden: of freshness, fecundity, and fruition.

JULY

by

Lanning Roper

July is an attractive month in the garden with its lingering bounty of roses, the bulk of the lilies, and the coming of age of a host of fuchsias, geraniums and annuals, which will give pleasure until frost. It is a month of long twilights when gardens are at their romantic best, or perhaps you, like myself, prefer the early mornings when the grass is cool with dew, and the blue of morning glories and the iridescent rainbow of poppies lift the spirits.

It is always difficult to list flowers in a given month. Lilacs or roses in London or Devon have probably finished flowering when the same varieties are just reaching their peak in East Anglia, Yorkshire or Scotland. This also goes for fruits and vegetables. Seasons vary, as we know only too well. Plants that should flower in June, may add weight and colour to the July border, and we occasionally see combinations of plants in flower that we have seldom seen before. However, the seasons have a curious way of catching up; a late spring may merge with a normal summer.

I like to cook, and so for me July is a gourmet's delight with strawberries, blackcurrants, the first raspberries, tender peas, courgettes, succulent carrots, French artichokes and a wide choice of fresh herbs to delight the palate.

One of my favourite dishes can be the byproduct of the thinnings from the rows of beetroots. The leaves and stalks are delicious if lightly cooked, coarsely chopped and served with plenty of butter and freshly milled pepper. If there are some young beets

32 The central axis of the walled garden at Penns in the Rocks, Sussex, with pear trees growing in beds of pink Rugosa roses, alternating with box and santolinas. *Alchemilla mollis* and rosemary grow in the foreground

as well, so much the better. A delicious soup can be made with young peas, pods and all, if boiled until tender with onion, parsley and a little mint in water or chicken stock. Obviously, the soup must be rubbed through a sieve or Mouli, and the purée bound with a roux, thinned with milk, seasoned and served either hot or cold with a little cream and freshly chopped mint. Baby young broad beans served hot with butter, liberally sprinkled with crisp diced bacon and a very light dusting of finely chopped thyme is a delectable light dish. Contrary to popular belief, baby carrots do not have as much flavour and are not as sweet as more mature ones. Don't pull them too early.

July is the month when butterflies hover over the long borders of lavender. The purple flower spikes just opening are ready for cutting and drying, along with scented-leaved geraniums, lemon verbena, rosemary and thyme. It's the month of summer pudding, pot-pourri, and sweet peas.

Roses play a major role in most gardens. I have a long list of favourite old roses with 'Celestial', 'Fantin Latour', 'La Reine Victoria', and 'Madame Isaac Pereire' crowding others for first place. There are also many newer roses which delight me, including hybrid teas, floribundas and polyanthas, although these distinctions are fast breaking down. Modern shrubs such as 'Cerise Bouquet', 'Constance Spry', 'Fritz Nobis' and the vinous-purple 'Chianti' are remarkably good value. Another of my favourites is 'Golden Wings', which flowers throughout the summer and combines so well with other plants. This exquisite single yellow rose with its long pointed buds combines happily with euphorbias, Nicotiana 'Lime Green', steely blue eryngiums, and Alchemilla mollis.

I find rose 'The Fairy' useful because of its spreading habit and large clusters of clear pink flowers, which follow the first flush of many other roses. Another treasure is 'Little White Pet', a charming dwarf form of 'Félicité et Perpétue'. These associate happily and both flower for a very long season. 'Ballerina', an apple-blossom-pink single hybrid musk, is another winner which

8 Above: The Long Border at Great Dixter
9 Below: The Horse Pond at Great Dixter – the most relaxing spot
in the whole garden

10 Left: The splendid rich blue of *Anchusa italica* 'Loddon Royalist'

11 Below: The little pink dog rose *Rosa rubrifolia* with its unique purply-grey leaves

12 Left: Charming, informal planting combining euphorbias, santolinas, geraniums and silvery verbascums against golden yew at the American Museum at Bath

13 Below: A corner of the formal rose garden at Bampton Manor, Oxfordshire, with standard Rose 'Ballerina' in borders that combine blue rue, purple sage and pink and blue lavender

14 Above: The mixed border at Elmstead Market, Colchester
15 Below: The pond surrounded by water-loving plants at
Elmstead Market

33 The paved terrace at Hall Place in Hampshire with the hybrid musk 'Penelope' flanking the gate to the rose garden. Pinks, thyme, marjoram and even self-sown hellebores soften the stonework

obligingly flowers later than the other musks. It can reach a height of five or six feet so give it plenty of room. Rose 'Yesterday' is rather like 'Ballerina' but with slightly smaller flowers of delicate pink shaded lilac borne in loose clusters. Butterflies and bees understandably love its honeyed fragrance. It grows to a metre or more and looks enchanting grouped near *Rosa rubrifolia* and in association with the other plants that I have mentioned. All these roses combine happily with lavenders, santolinas, blue rue, and purple sage in mixed borders for schemes providing low maintenance and long effectiveness.

Rosa rubrifolia is a superb species with foliage ranging from delicate silvery mauve to glaucous purple, starred with small single pink flowers in summer, and, in autumn, with a bounty of red fruits. It is a wonderful foil for other plants. In front of it I like to group the unusual new *Berberis* 'Rose Glow', *Fuchsia magellanica* 'Versicolor' and feathery silver *Artemisia* 'Lambrook Silver' or *A.* 'Powis Castle' for a harmony of subtle colour. *Rosa rubrifolia* is striking with dark wine-red cotinus or rhus, massed with clear pink or lilac floribunda roses. A group or two of *Rosa chinensis* 'Old Blush', in bloom for most seasons of the year, is a happy addition.

I have always had a great fondness for lilies. When I was a child in New England, where I spent my youth, the graceful *Lilium canadense* grew in fields near our house, and I have seen some of the other wild North American lilies in their native habitats. July is the peak month for lilies in our gardens. Whites, pale yellows, and pastel pinks are my favourites. The Madonna lily *(Lilium candidum)* was an early love, and fortunately proved less fickle when I was ten than it does today. I remember as a child the excitement aroused by the arrival from France in early September of shallow wicker hampers filled with fat white bulbs, packed in the gleaming husks of beechnuts, that rustled as they poured through my fingers. Plant the bulbs in September if you can get them as early as that, in full sun, on well-drained soil – preferably alkaline – with the nose of the bulb just below the surface of the soil.

Regale lilies are equally lovely and far more reliable, flowering for most of July. They are eminently satisfactory in pots or tubs in a city garden, as a clump or two can light up an all-green border. They are the flower arranger's dream, as every bud opens in water and the individual blooms last well. I am very fond of pale yellows, especially if there is a tinge of green. Clones such as 'Limelight' and 'Honeydew' are the answer to prayer, as are the huge trumpets, 'Green Dragon' and 'Black Dragon', named for the flush of colour on the buds and the reverse of the petals. For those who want an easy lily of a brilliant nasturtium-red with a

34 The bold form of Regale lilies, backed by eremurus and giant thistles, in
Vita Sackville-West's enchanting White Garden at Sissinghurst

hint of pink, 'Enchantment' is the answer. It's a great lily, and, unlike many, so healthy that it seems to be here to stay after thirty odd years of trial.

Martagons naturalise more happily than other lilies as is proven by the fine colonies in a number of woodland gardens. Best known are the fine stands in the wilderness garden of St John's College, Cambridge, usually at their best in mid-July. As they are native to southern Europe, extending over a vast area from Spain and Portugal across the Balkan Peninsula, parts of the Caucasus and much of European Russia, it is not surprising that they are both lime-tolerant and lime-loving.

The pendulous turkscap flowers vary greatly in colour from greenish pinks, pale purples and dusky mauves to deepest purple bordering on black *(L. martagon cattaniae* and *dalmaticum)*. My favourites are the whites, which stand out effectively in shadowy green shrubberies and woody glades. Martagons establish slowly, so don't be disappointed by a poor performance of newly planted bulbs for a year or even two.

Flowering trees play a large part in any garden. Spring sees the major flush of cherries, crabs, and magnolias. July is far more restrained. Perhaps the loveliest are the stewartias, which continue to flower in August. I treasure them for their habit, distinctive bark throughout the year, brilliant autumn colour, and flowers not unlike cup-shaped single white camellias. The Japanese *S. pseudocamellia*, the more shrub-like *S. malacodendron*, native to the South-East of the United States, and the handsome *S. koreana*, with rather more showy open flowers, are possible choices. Give them lime-free soil and semi-shade for good results.

Magnolia virginiana is surprisingly one of the lesser known magnolias, as it produces its creamy white, bowl-shaped flowers over a long season from June well into September, never admittedly in the spectacular fashion of the spring-flowering Asiatic species such as *M. stellata, wilsonii, campbellii, denudata* and the hybrid soulangianas, but in happy succession so that there are usually a few sweetly fragrant blooms among the attractive foliage. It likes a fairly moist position in a favoured position if it is to retain its semi-evergreen foliage through all or part of the winter. *Magnolia grandiflora*, the finest of the magnolias from the United States, is far more spectacular because of its great size as a tree in

35 The south terrace at Hill Barn House in Wiltshire, carefully planted for winter and summer effect with a yellow *Phlomis fruticosa* against *Magnolia grandiflora*, a Moroccan broom on the wall and rampant white roses on the gable end. Note the bands of cobbles in the paving

favoured locations, its huge glistening evergreen leaves with red-bronze indumentum on the under sides and huge, white, lemon-scented flowers, which appear in mid-July in a warm summer and last into the early autumn. In a sheltered position give it lots of room and grow it as a free-standing tree and not against a wall.

It is interesting how large a part yellow flowers play in the July colour scheme. The pineapple-scented Moroccan broom *(Cytisus battandieri)*, with its clusters of soft yellow pea-shaped flowers and silvery foliage, makes a free-standing small tree, or it can be trained against a warm wall, preferably near a blue ceanothus or a solanum for happy contrast. Late in July there is the Mount Etna broom *(Genista aetnensis)* with clouds of minute yellow flowers and delicate ferny foliage. Old specimens develop into graceful arching trees as much as twenty feet tall. I like to use this elegant tree in borders where height and light shade are needed. The shrubby *Genista cinerea*, a close relation of about half the size, with a pleasing harmony of small silky grey-green leaves and golden flowers, is one of the showiest of July-flowering shrubs, and, like the Mount Etna broom, it is very fragrant.

There is another spectacular yellow-flowered tree with the charming vernacular names Golden Rain Tree and Pride of India. Both are well chosen. *Koelreuteria paniculata* is a wide-spreading small tree, up to twenty or thirty feet tall, with handsome pinnate leaves that allow a pattern of filtered sunlight on the ground beneath, and panicles of flowers like golden torches in July and August. It likes a sunny position and is so rewarding when it flowers that it is worth the wait of a few years, as it may be shy of bloom when young.

Spanish broom *(Spartium junceum)* is even more spectacular because of its large, bright yellow, pea-shaped flowers in upright racemes. It can be grown as a free-standing shrub or trained against a fence or wall to form a curtain of gold. Its very sweet fragrance is an added asset. Prune it hard in late winter or early spring as it flowers on new wood. It makes a lovely background for summer-flowering ceanothuses such as the powder-blue 'Gloire de Versailles', or, better still, the brighter blue 'Henri Desfosse' or 'Topaz'.

I am partial to a yellow and white colour scheme, as the latter cools down the yellow. Masses of rose 'Iceberg' or the rugosa variety 'Blanc Double de Coubert', which flowers over such a long season, are effective when worked into the above scheme as are romneyas with their huge white poppy flowers with golden centres, which earn the name Poached Egg Flower. They are tricky to establish, but in a sunny position on good garden soil they will eventually spread luxuriantly. Plant them with big clumps of *Achillea* 'Coronation Gold', with the lower-growing *A.* 'Moonshine' in the foreground. Achilleas last in flower well into

August and, with hardy blue agapanthus for contrast of leaf shape and colour, make a striking plant association.

I have a weakness for clear yellow day-lilies, and an aversion to the orange. There are a number of cool lemon and golden varieties, some of them fragrant. They start flowering in June and last through July into August. Their arching strap-shaped leaves appear early in spring and give character to the border. 'Marion Vaughn', 'Jake Russell', 'Lark Song', 'Diamond Dust', 'Hyperion' and 'Whichford' are excellent large-flowered yellows. 'Golden Chimes' and 'Corky' are dwarf and small-flowered but very floriferous. Apricot, rose, melon, and lavender hybrids are being developed in America by the hundreds, but I still prefer the yellows. Day-lilies combine well with agapanthus; and groups of *Galtonia candicans*, with its tall stalks of drooping white flowers like enormous snowdrops, will add interest in late July and August.

Hydrangeas are not my favourite shrubs but I love the lacecaps. However, I associate these with late summer. *Hydrangea paniculata* 'Praecox', with its panicles of white sterile florets, is a fine shrub for July, and to my taste preferable to the larger more spectacular 'Grandiflora'. Two other large shrubs with big panicles of white flowers, *Sorbaria aitchisonii* and the even taller *S. arborea*, are very useful where an informal natural effect is desired. They are reminiscent of spiraeas and fit into settings where gunneras, rodgersias and other waterside plants create Rousseau-type landscapes.

Every garden has space for climbers. July sees a wealth of clematis in a variety of sizes and colours. I like them best when they scramble up, over and through roses, shrubs and even trees. A dark yew hedge makes a perfect foil. One of my special favourites is *Clematis* 'Perle d'Azur', a soft clear azure blue with graceful flowers of moderate size. It is a winner. I also love the smaller flowered *Clematis viticella* with its curtain of nodding purple flowers, and its hybrids including the pearly white 'Huldine' and the white and mauve 'Minuet'.

Turning to hardy perennials, herbaceous clematis are attractive but they need support. *Clematis davidiana* 'Wyevale' has clusters of clear blue scented flowers, reminiscent of the florets of a hyacinth, and handsome foliage. *Dictamnus albus (*or *D. fraxinella)*, known as Burning Bush, is another herbaceous plant deserving special mention. I love its foliage, its light purple or white flowers, and its very decorative seed pods borne in erect spikes. The leaves smell of lemon peel when you brush against them while weeding, and at night, a very still one, dictamnus is known to give off a volatile gas, that burns for an instant with a tiny blue flame. Plant dictamnus carefully and mark the position, as it sometimes disappears from view during the first season. It is slow to develop but in time will make a large clump in which you can take inordinate pride. Perhaps my enthusiasm is coloured by the remembrance of a sultry summer night, when I actually saw for the first and only time a tiny blue flicker.

Another hardy plant of childhood was monarda or, as we called it then, Bee Balm. The soft delicate colouring of 'Beauty of Cobham' with its dusky pink flowers, framed by gleaming purple bracts, gives me renewed pleasure each July and reaffirms my choice. The variety of my youth was 'Cambridge Scarlet', but to this day it is a plant which I have never used as I dislike the strong colour.

As you may have gathered, I rate fragrance very high. Therefore I want in my July garden annuals including night-scented stocks, the large white tobacco plant *(Nicotiana affinis)*, heliotrope, sweet alyssum, mignonette, *Dianthus* 'Loveliness', and the old-fashioned small-flowered dark purple sweet pea. Climbers must include white jasmine and honeysuckles, both the Late Dutch and the indispensable *Lonicera japonica* 'Halliana'. Rugosa roses and sweetbriar *(Rosa rubiginosa)* with its highly aromatic foliage must share honours with limes and late flowering philadelphus. *Philadelphus insignis* and *P. incanus* are two late fragrant species from very different parts of the world. The former is native to California; the latter to central China.

Rhododendrons that are fragrant and flower in July are few, but if there is room in your garden for several large ones and soil is

36 Late-flowering philadelphus scent the July garden

suitable, plant *R. auriculatum* or, better still, 'Polar Bear', a hybrid of it. Both are large shrubs or, in time, small trees with white fragrant flowers. 'Polar Bear' is a superb plant with huge white trumpet-shaped flowers in loose trusses. There is a hint of green in the throat of each flower and the rich fragrance is carried on the night air. This rhododendron is particularly beautiful at dusk. It starts to flower in July and often lasts well into August. There are two difficulties. It is a scarce plant and too often young shrubs are slow to produce flowers. Patience may be required on both counts.

If you live in a mild district grow the large flowered *R. crassum*, a tender species of the maddeni series, dark pink in bud, with white funnel-shaped flowers shaded pale pink with a rich fruity scent. It's also a good shrub for a cool conservatory or orangery.

The eastern North American Swamp Honeysuckle, *Rhododen-dron viscosum*, is an intensely fragrant white deciduous azalea, flowering in late June and July. It likes a cool moist position where it will not dry out. There are fine clumps in the Savill Gardens.

Every month has its special tasks and those for July are basically pleasant ones. The sowing of biennials for next year should have been done in May or June but if there are to be stocks of wall flowers, daisies like *Bellis perennis*, winter-flowering pansies and forget-me-nots for the spring, early July is the last chance in mild areas. In cold areas it's too late.

It's always a pleasure to plan ahead and to ring the changes. Why not have pink or white forget-me-nots as a change from the blues? There are lovely soft coloured wallflowers ranging from ivory and primrose yellow to pinks and dusky ruby reds. Fox-gloves, especially the creamy whites and apricots, are invaluable for semi-shade and for new schemes where height is needed quickly. Alas, it gets increasingly difficult to obtain selected colours. Can-terbury bells and sweet williams are standbys for cutting and garden display. I much prefer the simple old-fashioned single Canterbury bells to the rather blowsy cup and saucer varieties, but I seem to be in the minority, judging from the seed catalogues. Young seedlings sown earlier should be lined out to develop.

Another July task is the dividing and replanting of bearded irises. This should be done as soon as possible after they finish flowering. Early July is ideal. Discard the worn out central rhiz-omes, retaining the plump outer ones by cutting cleanly back to solid fleshy stock. Plant the rhizomes on the surface of the carefully prepared soil, preferably on a ridge, cover the roots and firm well. The upper surface of the rhizome should be very lightly covered. As the soil settles the upper surface will be exposed. Cut back the leaves either in the pattern of a fan or fishtail to reduce wind resistance and water the plants well.

As lilies begin to flower in early July, stake them carefully to support the heavy flower heads. After the main burst of bloom of roses in June and the first half of July, give your bushes a feed to encourage growth and a vigorous repeat flowering. Keep sweet peas well watered if weather is dry and do not allow them to set seed. This will ensure a long flowering season.

The pleasures of July are heightened by the arrival of the first of the spring bulb catalogues. They lie temptingly on the table, perhaps near a big bowl of sweet peas or apricot and pink Ligtu Hybrid alstroemerias. So strong is the pull of the garden next spring that I for the moment forget the bounty of summer. Such is the nature of gardeners.

AUGUST

by

Beth Chatto

If, in the early days of my gardening life, I had been asked to name a flower for each month of the year I would probably have replied something like this. January – snowdrops, February – crocuses, March – hellebores, April – daffodils, May – tulips, June – roses, July – lilies, August – dust, dead grass and black spot! Certainly I would have been appalled to be asked to enthuse about the garden in what is possibly the most disheartening month of the year. Or rather it can be, and used to be in my case.

Living as I do in the driest part of East Anglia, we are always concerned with drought. Desiccating winds following pathetically mean showers of rain, left-overs of downpours before the rain clouds reach us – are very much the pattern of our growing season. Even in wet summers our rainfall is still only average, between $1\frac{1}{2}$ and 2 inches a month. In this part of the country, the garden in August is often a sad sight, the grass burnt brown, early plants finished and cut down, leaving perhaps weary looking stands of mildewed phlox and michaelmas daisies. If you do plenty of bedding out followed by copious watering the picture can be brighter, but I prefer more permanent planting.

I am very fortunate that my garden at Elmstead Market, near Colchester, is situated in a shallow hollow between two farms. Because there is a wide range of soil conditions we have been able to make several different types of planting. We began about twenty years ago, bulldozing away the bramble tangles, tall

bracken and nettle beds, and found we had everything, including
dry hungry gravel, moist black silt, and sticky wet clay in the hollow where there ran a spring-fed ditch. Over the years the ditch
has been dammed and transformed into five large pools, set in
sloping green grass, reflecting the bog-loving plants that we have
grouped around them.

However, three quarters of my land is very dry, free-draining
gravel, and it was the need to find something which would furnish
this difficult situation for most of the year that started my great
interest in leaves. Once you stop waiting for plants to produce
flowers to hide their leaves – and begin to find how many exciting
shades of colour, not to mention variety of forms and textures
there are to be found in leaves – you find yourself designing with
foliage, and the flowers follow incidentally.

I am now often quite relieved with the coming of August for
the confusion of flowering plants to ebb away, and the new fresh
patterns of leaves to take over. Walking along one of my dry
sunny borders at this time of year, I enjoy stands of tall feathery
bronze fennel above silver mounds of santolina, with Miss
Willmott's ghost, *Eryngium giganteum*, seeded among them.
Perhaps the loveliest of the sea hollies, she opens green, but slowly
turns to a silver milky-blue. There are many eryngiums, some
very spiny and prickly, others with soft and exquisite lace-like
ruffs surrounding their central cones. Their deep indigo blue
colouring, silvered veining and metallic texture look well with
velvety carpets of *Stachys olympica*, or lambs' ears, as we called it as
children.

All the artemisias, and there are so many, improve as the
summer passes. Silky, feathery, almost white foliage glows in the
dusk of late summer evenings, and, together with the cistus
bushes, thymes and santolinas, fills the air with warm southern
scents. Among them little lizards rustle over the dry soil, seed pods
of euphorbias explode and pop, bees hum busily in the calamint
bushes. I thought my first plant of *Calamintha nepetoides* was a dull
little thing, but as summer fades into autumn these little plants

produce more and more clouds of tiny pale blue flowers until they are a charming sight, crowded and humming with honey bees. They look well in the herb border surrounded with golden or variegated thymes, and the matt-leaved sages. The golden sage, *Salvia officinalis* 'Icterina', is a lovely foliage plant with soft gold and green variegated leaves, brightest in late summer. I have never seen it flower. The purple-leafed sage has just finished flowering, spasmodically, and will continue to produce its velvety purple leaves, some splashed with pink or cream.

Looking across the Dry Garden at this time of year, with its background of grey and silver plants, the dominant flower colour seems to be yellow. Outstanding is the Mount Etna broom, *Genista aetnensis*, not nearly so commonly planted as Laburnum, I wonder why not. Just now it is a fountain, fifteen feet high and across, dripping with millions of tiny yellow pea flowers, while the sweet spicy scent drifts over the garden. At ground level, yellow is repeated with *Coreopsis verticillata*, and lovely sharp, almost luminous yellow in the daisy *Anthemis tinctoria* 'Wargrave'.

38 *Anthemis tinctoria*

Shrubby potentillas are there in creamy white, primrose yellow, soft tans and apricot. Cool contrast is provided for these warm colours with shades of blue and purple. Tumbling over a raised bed sheltered under a west wall is *Convolvulus mauritanicus*, a very superior bindweed which never becomes a nuisance; it is massed with shallow fluted saucers in a lovely rich blue. This warm raised bed is a novelty for me, providing in flat Essex somewhere for tumbling plants to trail and where tiny treasures can be placed at a level where it is easy to see and care for them. Two plants, not in the least tiny, are demanding attention against this wall just now. *Crepis incana* is covered with hundreds of rose-pink dandelion flowers on thin branched stems, about nine inches high; it is a delight. Further along *Penstemon isophyllus* has shot up tall elegant stems hung with vivid scarlet and pink tubular flowers.

For the large border the double and semi-double forms of Shasta daisy, *Chrysanthemum maximum*, will go on producing new flowers for weeks to come. And so too will the *Acanthus mollis*, already holding stately stems above its mounds of handsome shining leaves. They have such strong moulded flowers of a curious dull maroon, with a clean white frilly petticoat held out seductively to encourage some insect to enter and fertilise the large cherry-like seed pod that will eventually be formed.

More white flowers will be added with the summer hyacinths – *Galtonia candicans*. They seem such luscious plants to be flowering in August. Their well-fed bulbs send up tall strong stems heavy with drooping white bells. Much nearer the ground are the soft grey mounds of *Anaphalis triplinervis* which will be massed with bunches of small white papery everlasting daisies. I hang these upside down and when they are quite dry I fill a large bowl with them to bring summer into the house in winter.

Round the corner of the house below the west wall, and on slightly better soil is a surprising riot of rich growth. The purple leafed vine is mixed up with trails of *Eccremocarpus scaber* whose burnt-orange flowers are intertwined with the soft scarlet of the Cape figwort, *Phygelius capensis*. *Clematis tangutica* adds to the tangle, smothered with tiny lemon flowers, while bold contrast is made with the great white crumpled petals of *Romneya coulteri*, the Californian tree poppy. Looking from the house across this jungly border I have enjoyed a tall bush mallow, *Lavatera olbia* 'Rosea', massed with large rosy-mauve silken flowers – it should be a feature for several weeks to come.

If we leave the Dry Garden and go down a shallow flight of steps we shall come on to the cool grass of the lower garden and arrive by the ponds. Here is a different world. The impact of lush green growth around is almost overpowering. Huge upturned

39 *Gunnera manicata*

parasols of *Gunnera*, each leaf more than four feet across, intricately puckered and crinkled to form a frilled and fluted edge, are lifted above our heads on great thick stems covered with green prickles. Protected between these barriers stand the curious flower spikes or fruiting bodies. About two feet high, they consist of close-packed fleshy fingers or cones, covered with small green dots which ripen to become small orange seeds. Extraordinary that such a vast plant produces such ridiculously small seeds.

More dramatic foliage is provided by the great phormiums, or New Zealand flax, which can be plain, purple, or variegated, while a towering grass, *Miscanthus sacchariflorus*, is ten feet tall, its drooping strap-shaped leaves catching the light like a waterfall. For the really large water garden there is *Petasites japonicus*, the gigantic Butter-bur, which I have planted to cover the banks of the neighbouring farm reservoir at the end of my garden. This plant makes thick underground stems (disastrous in a small garden) fine for stabilising sloping sides which could be washed down by winter rain. The enormous round leaves make overlapping mounds which smother the toughest weeds. In spring the bare clay bank will be dotted with its curiously attractive flowers, demure posies of white heliotrope-like clusters surrounded by a ruff of primrose-coloured bracts.

Adding lightness to these architectural giants are such plants as Mr Bowles' golden sedge (a form of *Carex stricta*) – a lovely grass-like plant, like a bright golden sunburst overhanging the water's edge, and repeated across the pool by a dainty shrub which has golden leaves all the growing season. It used to be called *Spiraea opulifolia*, but now it is *Physocarpus opulifolius* 'Luteus'.

Too many flowers out at the same time can spoil the atmosphere of tranquillity by the waterside, but somehow there is a spaced effect, of colour coming and going, among the rich foliage. Most of the candelabra primulas and water iris are over now, but *Primula florindae*, the mealy Himalayan giant cowslip, is reflected in the dark water, with yellow musk nearby, and not far away the yellow is repeated in the tall *Thalictrum flavum* which holds fluffy masses of tiny yellowish-green flowers high above wax-blue leaves.

Astilbes are good in August, and especially I love the small ones like Sprite, which has finely cut bronze green foliage and wide airy sprays of shell pink flowers. More pink is provided by several meadow sweets. *Filipendula rubra* 'Venusta' runs about in the Bog

40 One of the moisture-loving daisies *Ligularia* 'Gregynog Gold'

Garden sending up six-foot stems topped with swirls of tiny pink flowers – like sticks of candy floss.

There is a race of moisture-loving daisies among which I find myself still confused. *Ligularia, Inula* and *Buphthalmum* – they are all handsome looking creatures, flowering and leafing well into late summer provided they are in good soil which does not dry out. I have at least three that are similar, yet not the same. One makes enormous basal leaves, dock shaped, which send up six-feet stems carrying wide heads of large yellow daisies whose petals are cut to narrow ribbons. Nearby, with similar foliage is a smaller version with orange-peel shredded petals, with a large central disc that goes brown with age. Finally by the waterside is silhouetted yet another, with impressive foliage and towering stem, up to eight feet high, narrowly set with green knobby buds which open out into a spire of smallish yellow daisies, and eventually make a gigantic seedhead – useful for decorating a large room.

Tapering spires are needed I think among rounded clumps like day lilies, or scented border phlox, both flowering now. Two I like specially. The first is *Lysimachia ephemerum*; it is, surprisingly perhaps, related to the modest little Creeping Jenny. However, this plant makes clumps of 4-foot stems elegantly set with blue-grey leaves and topped with neat spires of small white flowers. *Veronica virginica* 'Alba', faintly washed with lilac, creates a similar effect – the flowers set more closely on narrower spires.

41 The corrugated bluish leaves of *Hosta sieboldiana*

Both in my ponds, and in cool borders, in well-prepared sites, I grow several forms of *Zantedeschia*, which we know better as arum lily. Although they grow wild in South Africa, they can be grown here with some protection in winter. In natural ponds they are protected from frost when established in the deep mud floor, while in a border a thick covering of straw or bracken keeps them safe. The form known as 'Crowborough' is now at its best on the edge of one of my shrubberies. Few flowers have such purity of line, each single 'petal' rolled and spiralled like an old-fashioned sweet-bag. Beside it towers the green-flowered form, known as 'Green Goddess'. Standing tall as I am are enormous fluted funnels whose wide green tips disappear into ivory throats. The great leaves form a feature in themselves – indeed you have to look twice to spot the flowers among them.

After the sunny scented slopes of my Dry Garden and the lush watery scene by the ponds it is a pleasant change to walk along a wide grassy path beneath ancient oaks which form a boundary between my garden and the neighbouring farm. Here in the cool of trees and shrubs I have collected together shade-loving plants. The soil is black meadow silt, fairly water-retentive, and I have added to it compost and manure before planting. I use mulches of pulverised bark or straw to prevent germination of weed seedlings and help conserve moisture. Having said that, the soil does get pretty dry by August unless we are lucky enough to have a thunderstorm. However, provided I have remembered to put down slug bait, the hostas along this walk are now their magnificent best, especially forms of *Hosta sieboldiana* – they have beautiful corrugated bluish leaves, more than a foot long, almost as wide. They are unforgettable features, remaining so until October when they turn to transparent gold before the great piles collapse. The golden leafed raspberry, *Rubus idaeus* 'Aureus', runs about between the clumps of hostas; it never seems to grow much more than a foot or so tall, but it makes vivid golden ground cover and I especially like it around the base of my purple leafed hazelnut.

The general effect of this winding walk between two shady

borders is predominantly leafy, green with ferns, periwinkles, epimediums, and lots of *Euphorbia robbiae*. But those plants which are flowering, or berrying, now stand out, fresh and isolated, against the quiet background. *Actaea rubra* is one of these, doing much better in shade than elsewhere. It has made strong clumps of pretty spiraea-like leaves, topped with heavy clusters of small enamelled red berries. I am delighted too with something called *Coriaria japonica* which I admired at the Harlow Car Gardens in Yorkshire for its low sprawling branches set with handsome yellow tinted foliage in autumn. I obtained a seed and was eventually most surprised to see it, as now, loaded with clusters of waxy red berries set all down the branches, between the leaves. Elsewhere I have *Coriaria terminalis xanthocarpa*, a lengthy name for another fascinating shrub. Actually, although it makes a shrub-like plant, it disappears in winter, but sends up, like a fuchsia, wide branching stems which are now weighted down by long tapering spikes of orange translucent berries which are actually swollen flower petals enclosing little black seeds. It is amusing, if exasperating, to watch the cheeky blackbirds and thrushes jump from the terrace floor to reach the berries hanging tantalising above them, the branches being too slender to support the weight of the heavy birds.

In a more open space in my shady walk is a much admired type of cow parsley, *Selinum tenuifolium*. Above soft mounds of fresh, almost fern-like foliage float airy white parasols poised on dark struts which are lost in the fading light of evening. Pink and white astrantias look right among them. They have themselves a modest old-fashioned look, their clusters of tiny central florets being surrounded by a frill of bracts. Again I feel the need of a strong and sturdy accent to set behind these delicate looking plants and I have chosen *Phytolacca clavigera*, the Chinese poke weed. It makes many stout branches each carrying a thick upturned spike which is made up of closely packed cyclamen-pink small starry flowers. These have matured now into a poke or spike of berries, which will gradually turn black and juicy like elderberries, but which unlike them, are poisonous.

42 The airy white parasols of *Selinum tenuifolium*

I started this chapter by calling August a disappointing month; but on walking round in August I find far more plants looking attractive than I can possibly mention. Although I am fortunate to possess a piece of land with so many different types of soil condition I have learnt two very important lessons which have helped my gardening. The first is that most soils can be improved with time and effort. Secondly, plants need to be put, as far as possible, into the kind of site that Nature intended, and from this it follows that there is a plant for almost every kind of condition. So, when they are happy and thriving, in the right place in your garden, you too will be told 'You must have marvellous soil'.

SEPTEMBER

by

Graham Stuart Thomas

We are very blessed in this country. We can go into our gardens and find flowers in any month of the year; at any rate, except during periods of severe frost, I can always count on finding something in mine. A few hundred years ago this would not have been possible. In mediaeval and later times, most flowers were of the spring and early summer only. This becomes particularly apparent when planting gardens of those early periods, with plants which would have been in cultivation at the time. Few flowered after the end of June. But in those days thoughts and work were very much focused on the seasons, and great importance was given to fruits; their beauty and their uses were appreciated in season. There was no question of going to the local shop to buy fruit in every month; still less to get a potted chrysanthemum in bloom in spring. And in the garden our favourites like hydrangeas and Japanese anemones – both from the Far East – or the fuchsias, dahlias and nasturtiums – all from South America – and numerous annuals, were unknown. Roses flowered only at midsummer.

Because flowers are so beautiful, countless kinds have been brought home from abroad, and are surprisingly happy in our island climate. It might be worth adding here that this is what horticulture is all about. The transcendent beauty of flowers is something which is apt to be forgotten by young prospective gardeners, and also, I'm sorry to say, sometimes by their teachers. There would be no need to study what may be broadly called the science of horticulture were it not for the beauty of flowers, coupled of course with the beauty and use of fruit and vegetables. But it is the *beauty of flowers* which has made us want to have beautiful gardens. We should not forget it.

I hope you will all be enjoying your runner beans, your succulent calabrese, Brussels sprouts and cauliflowers during September. It is a month also of special interest from the fruit point of view. The late fruiting greengages and peaches are superlative, pears melt in your mouth and that notable plum 'Coe's Golden Drop' is ripening. The little red apple 'Devonshire Quarrenden' is losing its crisp juiciness but 'James Grieve' and 'Laxton's Fortune' are ready to take its place. Many apples fall and have to be stewed and for adding flavour I think there is nothing to beat blackberries. I have 'Oregon Thornless' trained over an arch; its fruit is large and luscious, and it is such a comfort not be torn by prickles. It is of quick and graceful growth and the leaves are deeply cut and fern-like; it is therefore an ornamental plant apart from its flowers and glossy fruits. In my estimation it surpasses other thornless varieties in quality and flavour.

There is nothing like picking your own fruit and eating it fresh from the tree, but many are deterred from planting fruit trees by the thought of huge old trees overshadowing everything, difficult to spray and prune, to say nothing of harvesting. But during the last half century or more our experimental stations have produced special rootstocks which will keep growth under control, and so compact pyramids and cordons are possible which are easy to manage and protect from the birds, bless them. The result is small apple and pear trees for small gardens. Reverting, though, to my earlier remarks, these prolific compact little plants have none of the beauty of a big old tree, particularly apples. There are few greater joys in a garden than the sight of a graceful old tree, with rough grey bark, and red apples shining through the foliage in September. Nor of course is there any tree so beautiful in spring bloom, particularly if you choose those with rosy red buds such as the excellent dessert 'Sunset' or culinary 'Lord Derby', with their fragrance and their dual value they stand high in my estimation, and do not give trouble with heaving, suckering roots as do the Japanese Cherries.

Apart from these gustatory delights, fruits of an ornamental kind will give colour and interest to a garden in September. The mountain ash or rowan, a native of Britain, has been supplemented by many species from China which bear lovely clusters of berries – admittedly loved by the birds, bless them again! – of different colours, white, yellow, pink as well as red, and towards the end of the month they are quite conspicuous. 'Joseph Rock' is a great joy because its butter-yellow berries are contrasted by foliage that turns gradually to shining maroon and red before dropping, while the small compact head of *Sorbus poteriifolia* displays good pink berries. For a white-berried kind for the smaller garden *S. cashmiriana* begins to catch our attention at the end of August when its bunches of marble-sized berries turn from green to snow-white. Very often, but not always, the birds leave yellow and white berries severely alone; presumably they are either colour-blind or possibly reckon they are not yet ready for eating. And while our own native spindle scarcely shows its pink berries until November, a species from North East Asia, *Euonymus sachalinensis*, has ruby-red berries the size of cherries, dangling from the shrubby growth in late August, and continues through September. It is a first rate contrast for *Eucryphia* 'Nymansay', a tall columnar evergreen bearing beautiful white flowers abundantly for a long period in our warmer counties. *Rosa moyesii* and its relatives are even more conspicuous, with long flagon-shaped heps of brightest orange-red. If I were to select one it would be the form raised long ago at Wisley called 'Geranium', because of its fresh green leaves, compact habit and brilliant large heps – to say nothing of its dazzling red flowers in June. But I will come to roses later on.

There are plenty of flowers for our September garden. Annuals and bedding plants are by no means over; the hardy fuchsias and hydrangeas are still full of flower. I admired some of the newer

44 The abundant white flowers of *Eucryphia glutinosa*

hardy varieties in the Fuchsia Trial at Wisley and decided I must add 'Sealand Prince' and 'Paula Bayliss' to my clumps of 'Mrs Popple' which has the usual combination of crimson petals and purple skirt. Their colours are pink and lilac, and scarlet and lavender respectively. And, as a crimson and white counterpart to the little bushy 'Tom Thumb', there is 'Lady Thumb'. They make a delightful pair in beauty and in name. These are all what one would call large-flowered fuchsias, though the little dwarfs have rather smaller blooms. They are far removed from the wild type, *F. magellanica*, introduced from South America in the early nineteenth century, so much a part of old cottage gardens with their abundant small flowers hanging like a crimson fringe below the arching branches until frosts put an end to production. One of the most free of bloom is known as 'Thompsonii'; it is of upright growth and makes a delightful summer hedge.

Even so, for me, one fuchsia outshines all the rest. It is 'Gracilis Versicolor', of lovely graceful growth. It has small crimson flowers with the usual purple skirt, but the foliage makes an unforgettable September picture. In shade it is pale jade green, in sun it is of the same tint but shot delightfully with rosy copper. I have had it outside for years and it is bone hardy.

Michaelmas Daisies belong mainly to October, but one hybrid starts flowering in early August and continues till all are over. It is *Aster × frikartii*, and its best form is one called 'Mönch', meaning the Monk. Its large, regular, long-rayed flowers are of clear lavender-blue. I should not like to be without it; in fact I rank it as one of the six best herbaceous plants – but don't ask me for the names of the other five! On good soil it will achieve a height of four feet, and needs only the minimum of support. In the foreground I have a plant of an even longer flowering period – *Polygonum affine*. It is worth searching for a good form such as 'Darjeeling Red' or the more compact 'Donald Lowndes'. The little pink spikes turn to a deeper colour as they age. I think these will both be neglected when 'Superbum' becomes better known. I obtained it from a German nursery and it is really quite startling:

for weeks on end the flower spikes appear, at first almost white, turning gradually to crimson. One of the added attractions of these varieties is the rich warm brown that the carpet of leaves retains through the winter. It is really the long-lasting plants like these that form the basis for colour schemes late in the year together with plants of silvery foliage, such as the santolinas or cotton lavenders, species of *Artemisia*, lambs' ears and others.

I think the floral year provides no more beautiful flower – nor, indeed, a more beautiful plant – than the Japanese anemone. It is so stately, with good foliage all summer, and for several weeks gives us bowl-shaped blooms on tall stems. Scent is, sadly, lacking, but it has really every other attribute. The ordinary single white known as *Anemone* × *hybrida* 'Honorine Jobert' is as beautiful as any, the single pink running it close, and there are semi-double varieties from white to deep old-rose colouring. I have a particularly soft spot for the semi-double 'Prince Henry', raised in Germany in 1902, which is about the darkest in colour, and paler 'Queen Charlotte' is even older; but then, on further thinking, I return to the singles. Apart from the two old originals, my choice would include 'September Charm' in warm pink of two tones. They will thrive in sun or shade but are usually more free of flower and compact when grown in sun. The idea that hardy perennial plants more or less stopped after the July and August glory of the herbaceous border no longer holds, now that we are beginning to look around for flowers of other shapes than the ubiquitous, though beautiful, daisy-flowers of *Helenium, Anthemis* and the like.

Take for instance that Japanese dignitary *Kirengeshoma palmata*, whose yellow shuttlecock-like flowers hang from ebony calyces over handsome leaves. If you don't like plants that arch and droop, choose instead *K. koreana*, an erect plant now getting better known and almost identical otherwise to the normal species. The petals of both are thick and soft, like chamois leather. I could not suggest a more lovely companion for it than the Swiss Willow Gentian, *Gentiana asclepiadea*, in rich, true blue and for those who love the rare forms there are white and pale blue variants. These

45 & 46 Above: The shuttlecock flowers and handsome leaves of *Kirengeshoma palmata* go beautifully with *Gentiana asclepiadea* (left) the Swiss Willow Gentian

species of both genera are long-lived and easy when once established in a cool moist spot. On the other hand, for a hot sunny position, don't overlook the so-called Californian fuchsias, species of *Zauschneria*, short plants with brilliant scarlet tubular flowers. In *Zauschneria cana* the scarlet of the flowers is contrasted by silvery grey foliage. It is in beauty like the others for weeks.

The Autumnal Equinox falls on 23 September and often the weather is changeable and blustery at times, even cold, but the September in one's memory always seems to have had a couple of weeks at least of still, sunny weather. There is often a feeling of pause in the air, a last spell of summer, despite the shorter days. If rain does fall, it is the ideal time for dividing and planting heucheras, pyrethrums, phloxes and doronicums, but on warm sunny days a rich fragrance is given by the now large plants of sweet white *Alyssum* in the paving, the tobacco plants and mignonette, and the odd plants of heliotrope which one should always grow in a tub or pot near to the garden seat.

Butterflies sip the nectar from many late flowers – notably lots of the daisy family, and the flat pink heads of *Sedum spectabile*. The butterfly's August feast, the modern buddleia varieties, are mostly over, but the invaluable small-growing *Buddleia fallowiana* continues to produce its smaller arching sprays throughout the month, while through the summer and into late autumn we have the added attraction of the grey-white felted leaves. It needs a warm sunny position and the white form, 'Alba', is the one most usually seen. Grouped with a few plants of the hardy shrubby plumbago in the foreground it can make an unforgettable picture; this plant has to be ordered under the tongue-twisting name of *Ceratostigma willmottianum*. Except in the warmest of gardens it dies to the ground in winter, but wiry stems grow up carrying heads of pure cobalt blue flowers. In warm Septembers you may also be favoured with a visitation of humming-bird hawk-moths whose long tongues reach the nectar in the tiny tubular throats of the flowers.

This brings me to other shrubs. So many people seem to think

16, 17 & 18 The colourful fruits of autumn: the hips of *Rosa moyesii* 'Geranium' (top left); the white berries of Sorbus cashmiriana (top right) seen against the foliage of *Rosa rubrifolia* and below *Sorbus reducta*

19 & 20 Left: The exquisite little *Colchicum agrippinum*, freckled like a meadow fritillary. Below: *Liquidambar styraciflua*, the North American sweet gum

21 & 22 Opposite above: The unusual branch colours of *Salix* Opposite below: Early November leaves – both photos from Valerie Finnis' garden.

23 Left: A fruiting stem of the winter cherry or Chinese Lantern – *Physalis alkekengii*

24 Below: The magnificent snow gum *Eucalyptus niphophila*

that shrubs only flower during the first half of the year, but September has its own specialities. For fragrance, choose *Clethra tomentosa*, a late-flowering form of the Sweet Pepper bush, whose creamy white spikes continue for a long time, often into October. It prefers a lime-free soil and is a great treasure.

There are several species and hybrids of *Caryopteris*, all appreciating warm sunny positions. The best known is *Caryopteris × clandonensis*, which gives the effect of a brilliant lavender in bloom. The leaves are aromatic, too. The original hybrid is named 'Arthur Simmonds' after the raiser, but for deeper coloured flowers we might choose 'Ferndown' or 'Kew Blue'.

Again with aromatic leaves most of the rich yellow, shrubby hypericums or St John's Worts are at their best in August, but I should not want to be without the lighter yellow of *Hypericum hookeranum* in September. It will grow as much as six feet in height but can be kept smaller by spring pruning. *H. × moseranum* is a hybrid St John's Wort which flowers continuously from July until autumn. It is of shorter stature than most, annually achieving a foot or two. Though quite hardy at the root, it is apt to die down in cold winters. The great bunch of warm orange stamens enhances the broad yellow flowers.

If you like the somewhat heady fragrance of privet in July, as I do, give a thought to a Chinese semi-evergreen species, *Ligustrum quihoui*, which is extremely elegant with large, open sprays of tiny white flowers. I think perhaps it is the ideal graceful companion to the shrubby Mallow or *Hibiscus syriacus*, a stout erect shrub which repays the same sort of cultivation and pruning that you would give to a Hybrid Tea rose – though there are many old bushes about the country which flower well without much attention. They thrive, all of them, and flower best in the warmer, drier parts of this country; they are great favourites in France. Perfectly hardy, they seem to have what we might call a cautious approach to the English spring and start into growth very late. 'Mauve Queen' is the best in the typical colour, but selection over many years has resulted in a fine range of tints such as 'Woodbridge' in light crimson, 'W. R. Smith', pure white, several of blush tint, and the glorious 'Blue Bird'. The colours of all except 'W. R. Smith' are offset by glistening maroon and dark crimson centres. These are all single-flowered; the doubles are not so satisfactory in our variable climate. I think few shrubs at any time of the year can surpass them when in full bloom, and there is no blue-flowered shrub of such splendour as 'Blue Bird'.

I'm sure you are wondering when I'm going to return to the roses. Spring flowers come and go, and as the splendid bearded irises fade, then does the crown of the year arrive, and the roses are upon us. The roses I specially like are the old-fashioned types, the old French roses, favourites of the last century. A hundred years ago they were beginning to be neglected for the earliest of what we may call the modern strains – the Hybrid Perpetuals. Their neglect continued. Though the old French Gallicas, including the Red Rose of Lancaster, the Damasks, the White Rose of York and the Centifolias and Moss Roses flower only once, at midsummer, there is nothing like them in horticulture, in shape, colour or fragrance, and I like to think that the come-back they have staged over the last thirty years or so has ensured their future. Fortunately we need not be without them altogether in our September garden. The old Autumn Damask, perhaps deriving from Roman days, and some other old hybrids, especially of the Portland and Bourbon groups, combine all the unique qualities of the old French Roses with the extra bonus of a second flowering in September. And so we can plant the Portland varieties 'Comte de Chambord' and 'Jacques Cartier' knowing we shall enjoy a delicious second crop of true old French rose shape. I don't think lovers of these delights realise this fully, though they have certainly taken to heart many of the Bourbons. Never earlier in the year do we get *their* finest blooms; they are reserved for later. The second crop from carmine 'Madame Isaac Pereire' and its paler sport 'Madame Ernst Calvat' surpass themselves when the cooler nights arrive. Anyone who has not gazed into the dense array of petals, and drunk himself giddy with the wonderful perfume, has not savoured all

47 Graham Thomas' former garden in Surrey

that a rose can give. The old roses, it should be noted, are not at their best till full blown, which cannot be said of many moderns.

The blush 'Souvenir de la Malmaison' is again superlative in September, likewise its nearly single sport 'Souvenir de St Anne's'. But be sure you get the bush 'Malmaison' and not the climber. It is seldom out of flower from summer till autumn, whereas the climber is a big awkward grower with a long flowerless interval. Unlike many other strong shrubby roses of the older classes, these two take time to build into a bush some four feet high and wide.

Bourbons seem to go in pairs. The lilac-pink 'La Reine Victoria' and its blush sport 'Madame Pierre Oger' are both exquisitely shaped, flowering continuously, with rounded flowers composed of shell-like petals, borne on fairly upright bushes.

And as for 'Reine des Violettes' raised in 1860, it is bluer than any modern rose. It begins to open to a rich violet-purple but when fully expanded, it presents a wonderful array of closely-ranged petals of soft parma violet, with a super fragrance. It is one of the older roses whose flowers, so packed with petals, keep the central ones curved inwards producing what we call a button-eye. To get it to perfection, give it your best cultivation; it will make a good shrub of about five foot.

I think you will need a sunny wall to get the best out of 'Céline Forestier' – and what a best it is! Raised a hundred and thirty-six years ago, it is as free of its flowers as any modern rose. Its exquisite light yellow flowers are filled with petals and have an almost overpowering fragrance. It is one of the Noisette group to which 'Alister Stella Gray' belongs. This can be grown as a climber or large shrub. It was a favourite with my father who always chose one of its soft yellow buds for a buttonhole – for its sweetness. These two yellows in particular inherit their extreme sweetness from the rare climbing species *Rosa moschata*, whose single white flowers do not appear much before August and continue till autumn. But perhaps your garden is quite small – if so, choose little 'Perle d'Or' in soft apricot, and the delicate pink of 'Cécile Brunner'. These tiny fragrant flowers are the essence of roses in miniature, on bushes that seldom exceed three feet, and are seldom out of flower.

I suppose one inevitably thinks of the year's approaching end in September. The month is however a beginning as well as an end, because it is planting time for spring flowering bulbs. Bulbous plants flower at all seasons of the year and the autumn-flowering kinds need planting in summer, by the end of July if possible. It is a lovely moment when the first Neapolitan cyclamens appear, pink or white, from the bare earth. They seem to thrive in sun or shade in quite rooty dry places under trees and shrubs. They are best established, by the way, from pot-grown, rooted plants, and not from the dry corms. Their grey-green marbled leaves, which appear after the flowers, remain in beauty – great beauty – until late spring, by which time the small spherical seed pods on their coiled spring-like stalks will be ripe for gathering and sowing. That is, if you get there first, for ants love to cart them away for the sake of their sweet skins.

Like them, crocuses flower before their foliage grows, and different sorts will flower from now until April. There are genuine *Crocus* species, such as *speciosus* and *kotschyanus (C. zonatus)*, but, also known as autumn crocuses, are the colchicums whose leaves, of giant proportions, do not appear, either, until spring. While the crocuses are in shades of lavender and lilac, most of the colchicums are mauve-pink in colour, even near to crimson in *Colchicum speciosum* 'Atrorubens', with a superb white, *C. speciosum* 'Album', of tulip-like proportions. I always think it a little unfair to complain about the size of the leaves of colchicums. They provide rich greenery in spring before almost anything else does and, to me, are therefore valuable as companions for daffodils, in grass or in borders. And if they have lilies such as the September flowering *Lilium speciosum*, so fragrant and so beautifully shaped – or summer hyacinths *(Galtonia candicans)*, planted among them you will achieve a second flowering period from the same spot.

And so the garden year proceeds; September is often a lovely month, a meeting place for late summer and spring-like blooms.

OCTOBER

by
Wilfrid Blunt

Let me make it plain, right at the start, that I am now nearly a hundred years old. Horticulturally speaking, that is: I am aware that *Who's Who* states that I was born barely a stone's-throw after the death of Queen Victoria; but they say that one is *as old as one feels*, and when it comes to *practical* gardening I *feel* a nonagenarian.

I have always called a spade a spade; but for many years past I have bolted at the mere sight of one. And is not October the first of the Months of the Spade – the month when one ought to start trenching and double-trenching, planting bulbs, and doing back-aching things all day to the herbaceous border? In short, though I have always loved flowers, I have always disliked all gardening involving much in excess of a little dead-heading at chest level.

Gardens, like children, are delightful – in moderation. But have any of your own, and in these days, when full-time gardeners and nurses, even if procurable, are beyond the means of most people, an almost ceaseless round of breeding, feeding and weeding is the lot of those who create or procreate them. I prefer to enjoy the gardens of others, who are always eager – at times almost too eager – to show one every rarity; while as a schoolmaster I found pleasure for thirty-six years in the company of the young of others, and was even slightly paid for doing so.

True, I *have* a garden – of a sort – here at the Watts Gallery, and a gardener-cum-custodian with multifarious duties and obli-gations. But Watts, whose tastes and prejudices I must now respect, favoured the undisciplined garden: that awkward kind of compromise, that 'sweet disorder', which would today be called 'a just, honourable and lasting solution' of the insoluble conflict between guerilla weeds and cultivated plants. Watts would never let his gardener cut back the brambles or even remove a dead tree. So when I speak in glowing terms of some plant or other, do not rush down from London to see it; the Royal Horticultural Society's Garden at Wisley is ten miles short of Compton, and you are much more likely to find it there.

The danger the publication of ill-considered enthusiasm may lead to was very forcibly brought home to me when, long ago now, for a year or two I ran the gardening column in the *Sunday Times*. One October I had extolled the beauty of *Tulipa fosterana* (then called *fosteriana*), and recommended, with a journalist's gush, its immediate purchase and planting on a massive scale: 'If you can only afford a dozen, then buy a dozen. If you can afford a hundred, buy a hundred. But if you can afford a thousand, when May comes you will bless me.' I had myself bought, for my cat-run at Eton, half a dozen bulbs, one of which was to forget to put in an appearance. So I was not a little embarrassed when in the following spring the secretary of an Essex ladies' gardening club announced her intention of bringing two coachloads of its members to see my tulips at the height of their glory.

But to return to October. My predecessors in this book have, of course, already snapped up the 'good' months – those months when owners of gardens have them photographed for inclusion in horticultural magazines: 'My iris border in June; in the foreground a riot of the elegant and delicately perfumed *Dianthus* "Triumph of Tooting Bec",' and so on. One is never shown 'My iris border in October'. However, to queer the pitch of those who are soon to follow me I would mention that you sometimes *can* see irises in *my* garden in October, for in six of the nineteen years I have been at Compton – and I keep careful records of my special pets – I have had my first stylosas (as I still prefer to call *I. unguicularis*) in flower before that month was out; 1961 actually produced a couple on

1 October. Why this Mediterranean treasure – which, incidentally, grows almost down to sea level in its native habitat – should appear positively to enjoy our English winters passes my comprehension, though admittedly its unopened buds do protest and deliquesce when caught by the frost. I have it in two shades of mauve and in white, and one plant of a bootlace-leaved, very dark, streaky-bacon form which I collected at Olympia, and which I dare say is really *Iris cretica*; it often produces deformed flowers.

Early October usually also sees the fag-end of the colchicums (pronounced correctly, 'cŏl'kicums') and the peak of the autumn crocuses. I have had a passion for *Colchicum autumnale* ever since I first met it in its thousands in Bavarian meadows fifty years ago. (Why on earth is it so expensive to buy?) My German hostess announced at breakfast on the first morning, 'I've put a few Naked Maidens in your bedroom.' I did not then know that *Nackte Mädchen* was the German name for them, and replied '*Vielen Dank*' in a tone intended to combine gratitude with surprise and mild embarrassment. They earn this name for flowering in the absence of their leaves, which make a rather over-aggressive appearance in the summer. In parts of England, where they are also native, they are called 'naked boys' or 'autumn crocuses'; the latter is misleading in that they belong to the Lily family whereas the true autumn crocus, like all crocuses, belongs to the Irises. The colchicum, incidentally, is highly poisonous, killing (according to Dioscorides, in John Goodyer's splendid seventeenth-century translation) 'by choking, like to ye mushrumps' – by which I take it he means poisonous fungi. The French call it *tue-chien* or *mort-au-chien* – dog-killer; but alas! I cannot say that I have noticed any appreciable falling-off in the number of my neighbours' dogs.

I still prefer the common *Colchicum autumnale* to all the exotic hybrids such as 'Waterlily' – a marvel, says a certain nurseryman's catalogue, 'which should be seen to be appreciated'; this goes for most flowers. I like to have just a few of the vulgar kind in a small tumbler on my window-sill, where they give me more pleasure than whole bucketfuls of Constance-Sprying. Nor let me over-

look the exquisite little *Colchicum agrippinum*, freckled like our
meadow fritillary, which calls for nothing larger than a sherry
glass.

No less lovely are the true autumn crocuses, of which *Crocus
speciosus* is undoubtedly the gem. It comes from Asia Minor
and thereabouts – in fact, its range extends from Eastern Europe
to north-eastern Iran – turning our autumn into a simulacrum
of spring and spreading obligingly till – and I quote the same
nurseryman again – 'it produces carpets and patches of blue
quite as frolic and rich as those of English bluebells'; yet it still
deserves individual observation, and should not be dismissed as
merely a patch of a frolicsome blue carpet.

If, like me, you find that plants with centuries of history and
legend behind them have a special fascination that parvenus lack
(for example, *Lilium candidum* as compared with *L. regale*), then
you cannot dispense with the saffron crocus *(Crocus sativus)*. With

49 The saffron crocus, *Crocus sativus*

its sturdy orange-red stigmata thrust beyond the lips of its purple chalice, it is, however, more than deserving of a place in its own right. There is no space to do more than hint at its long history: a mention in the Bible (*Song of Solomon* iv.14) and many references to it (as *krokos*) in Homer and the works of other Greek authors; the burning at the stake together with their tainted wares, in fifteenth-century Nuremberg, of sellers of adulterated saffron; and above all the famous account in Hakluyt of the alleged intro-duction of saffron into England:

It is reported at Saffron Walden (in Essex) that a pilgrim proposing to do good in this country stole a head of Saffron, and hid the same in his palmer's staffe which he had made hollow before of purpose, and so he brought the root into this realme with venture of his life, for if he had bene taken by the law of the country from whence it came he had died for the fact.

It may be remembered that an exactly similar story is told about the introduction of the silkworm into the West from China.

Incidentally, according to the three hundred pages of Johann Ferdinand Hertodt's *Crocologia* (Jena, 1670), saffron is (I gather, for I have not dared to read it) a very handy plant to have around; for used in conjunction with powdered swallows' nests, myrrh, aloes, dragon's blood, the fat of the mountain mouse and other such readily accessible ingredients, there are few human ailments that it cannot cure. In short, 'A saffron a day keeps the doctor away.'

There are other autumn crocuses almost equally charming: the little Syrian *Crocus ochroleucus*, for instance – white with a golden throat – that often battles on well into November, as does also *Crocus longiflorus* from southern Italy and Sicily, which smells of primroses. Corms of all these should, of course, be ordered by the beginning of August at the latest.

I also very much like *Sternbergia lutea* – the nearest that autumn can provide to the yellow crocus of spring though in fact it is, as

50 *Sternbergia lutea* – the nearest that autumn can provide to the yellow crocus of spring

examination soon makes evident, actually a daffodil. The trouble is that it doesn't much care for me, and certainly never flowers as freely here as the bulb-merchants lead one to expect. (Indeed, I sometimes wonder how one or two of these firms would fare under the Trades Description Act; I will gladly give five pounds to any charity Messrs. X care to name, if they can convince me that *Iris susiana* is 'of easy culture' in south-eastern England.)

The Guernsey Lily *(Nerine sarniensis)*, and *Nerine bowdenii* – both natives of South Africa in spite of the common name of the former – flower terrifically, I observe, for some of my neighbours. There is a cottage garden in our village which looks in October regrettably as if a cartload of raspberry ices had been tipped over the fence. The curious circumstances in which the Guernsey lily acquired its misleading name is told, though rather inaccurately, in the 1795 volume of *Curtis's Botanical Magazine*: 'A Dutch or English ship, it is uncertain which, coming from Japan with some of the roots of this flower on board, was cast away on the island of Guernsey. The roots were thrown upon a sandy shore, and so by the force of the winds and waves, were soon buried. There they remained for some years, and afterwards, to the great surprise and admiration of the inhabitants, the flowers appeared in all their pomp and beauty.' It only remains to add that the Guernsey lily is *not* a native of Japan, and the bulbs must have been taken on board at the Cape. The Jersey Lily (Lillie Langtry), though she flourished in many beds, is of no horticultural interest.

But enough of bulbs and corms. October usually heralds the advent of what my mother always referred to as 'the tints' – that magic moment when Midas touches the leaves of many deciduous trees and shrubs and turns them to every known and unknown shade of gold. 'A question often asked of the staff at Wisley,' wrote its Director, Mr Brickell, 'is: "What is the best time to visit the Garden in order to see the autumn colour at its peak?"' Opting for the last two weeks of October and the first in November, he adds a predictable codicil:

As with most forecasting of natural events, a definite answer can seldom be given and a fairly wide margin of error should be allowed. Change in leaf colour is no exception, depending as it does on several interrelated factors, including the prevailing weather – itself far from certain – the acidity of the cell sap and the concentration of the various pigments remaining after the breakdown of chlorophyll prior to leaf-fall.

The cause of this change of colour is explained in yet more scientific language by another botanist. It is due, he says, to the disorganisation of the layer of parenchymatous cells lying just outside the cork layer formed across the base of the petiole by the meristematic activity of the phellogen, or bark cambium.

But to return to my mother, who also would not have understood this. Every autumn my mother would religiously gather great boughs of beech for decorating the drawing-room, but I always felt that her method of preparing them for their long winter vigil among the framed photographs on the grand piano left something to be desired. It was her custom to place them under the various rugs and carpets in the hall and passages, which rendered progress over them perilous and from which ordeal they finally emerged flat as pancakes. I never succeeded in persuading her to try glycerine.

Beeches and sycamores provide glory enough for most of us, but obviously there are some more refined pleasures for the connoisseur. The North American *Liquidambar styraciflua*, or sweet gum – good forms of which (and one must be careful when choosing a specimen) laboriously paint each leaf a different shade of gold, orange, crimson, scarlet and vinous purple – is to my mind the most amazing. And here let us pause a moment to bless the botanists for choosing, and retaining, a comprehensible generic name and a descriptive specific epithet: *liquidus* in Latin means 'liquid', and *ambar* is 'amber'. *Styraciflua* means producing storax, or fragrant resin – which it does.

The first known reference to this remarkable tree is rather delightful: a witness of a ceremonial meeting between Cortez and Montezuma relates that after the Emperor had dined 'they presented to him three little canes, highly ornamented, containing liquidambar with a herb they called tobacco, and when he had sufficiently viewed and heard the singers, dancers and buffoons he took a little of the smoke out of one of these canes'.

That enterprising botanical Bishop of London, Dr Henry Compton, who had several correspondents in the New World, introduced the American liquidambar (for there are Asiatic species also) into England in the 1680s and grew it in his garden at Fulham Palace. For this one can easily forgive him for having earned the reputation of being the dreariest episcopal preacher of his generation.

Another (but in my opinion rather overrated) relation of the liquidambar, *Parrotia persica*, is also grown more for its autumn colour than for the little clusters of red flowers that appear on its bare branches in the spring. It is a substantial tree from Iran and the Caucasus, with a tiresome tendency to spread sideways when you want it to grow upwards, and was named after a German naturalist and traveller, Dr Johann Jacob Parrot, who in 1829 first climbed the 17,000-foot Mount Ararat. I presume it was he who discovered the Persian witch hazel (as it is sometimes called); it was a pity that he failed to discover Noah's Ark.

Exciting also are the maples (especially some of the Japanese species), the dogwoods, and various kinds of rhus, prunus and azaleas. There are vines and Virginia creepers; and one should not forget such of the innumerable trees and shrubs whose fruits have so far escaped the greed of birds: the exciting seed-pods of some of the peonies, clematises and irises and of the strawberry tree *(Arbutus unedo)* and spindle *(Euonymus europaeus)*, for example. 'Conkers' revive happy childhood memories, as do also the quite unrelated Spanish chestnuts that we collected and roasted on the hob, or bought, piping hot, for tuppence a bag from a vendor at the street corner. But there is a heavy price to be paid for so much bounty. Nature, the greatest litter-bug of all, is preparing to strip the trees of their glory, leaving man, namely my successor in November, to sweep it up and burn it or convert it into compost.

Usually the first *real* frost – the kind that kills the dahlias 'at a stroke' (as Sir Harold Wilson would put it) – delays its appearance at least until the end of October; therefore the herbaceous border, though beginning to look a bit tatty, probably continues to make quite a brave show. The principal ingredients of most autumn borders are familiar to all gardeners: michaelmas daisies (which the botanists call *Aster*), asters (which they call *Callistephus*), chrysanthemums and dahlias in endless varieties; fuchsias still going strong; various rudbeckias; *Ceratostigma*, both *willmottianum* and *plum-*

51 The undisciplined woodland garden at Compton with its mass of foxgloves – the 'sweet disorder' that Watts would have approved of . . .

baginoides; statice, golden rod, sedums . . . the list is endless. Against a south-facing wall there may also well be *Amaryllis belladonna, Salvia neurepia* (or whatever it is called this week), *Schizostylis coccinea* (the Kaffir lily), and perhaps, under some chosen tree, a handful of pink or white *Cyclamen hederifolium* (syn. *C. neapolitanum*).

I frankly admit that I like gardens in spring and autumn better than in high summer. Gardens are usually said by their owners to be 'at their best' when they are as congested as the London Underground in the rush hour. In general I don't care for surfeits; in fact in many ways I really prefer individual flowers to gardens. But here I make an exception of the area in front of the loggia which gives access to the Curator's house at the Watts Gallery. When I first came to Compton in 1959 I bought, for ten shillings each, eight very large tubs which I painted turquoise and fill annually with the brightest, vulgarest cascading geraniums, begonias, petunias, snapdragons and miscellaneous half-hardy annuals that I can acquire, and let them clash; it is rather fun shocking the visitors, though I usually have to evacuate the tubs, murdering their inhabitants when still in full splendour, in order to allow wall-flowers (Suttons' 'Persian Carpet') to be planted. But now the tubs are disintegrating, one by one, and are today too expensive to replace. Those that remain have about the same life expectancy as their owner, and I shall leave it to my successor to deal with the problem.

There is much to be said for autumn, and – since the introduction of central heating – for winter too. As the days shorten and that blessed moment comes when they put the clocks forward – or do I mean back? – one can, without a guilty conscience, draw the curtains early and sit indoors with one's thoughts and one's books and write – stuff such as this, for example. On my table one exquisite, inarticulate spray of winter jasmine; on my knees my almost equally inarticulate, beloved cat. Blessed silence! In short – like the daffodil or the hedgehog, I kind of hibernate.

NOVEMBER

by

Valerie Finnis

I was looking the other day at a gardening book which had lists of plants flowering in the different months, and I was rather surprised to see that the November list was the shortest. But of course there is a lot more to a garden than just flowers, and I certainly do not regard November as a dull month. For one thing it never seems able to make up its mind whether it is the first month of winter or the last month of autumn and can be full of surprises, and I'm not sure that I don't really rather look forward to it. It has its highlights like any other month, but before I begin to talk about my special November ones I had better tell you something about my garden, or, I should say, *our* garden, as I share the work with my husband.

It is in Northamptonshire, definitely one of our colder and drier counties, and we call it a 'home for plants' rather than a garden. There is no colour scheme or design about it; in fact, a garden architect once called part of it a maze! It is in four sections: a small sheltered bit against the house; then, up some steps, an oblong piece, about seventy by twelve yards, enclosed on the two long sides by low stone walls where I have most of my raised beds for small hardy plants and bulbs and grow my fruit and vegetables. Adjoining this is a large walled yard with my potting shed and more raised beds. Then you go through a gate into the 'maze' – about two acres of trees and shrubs and lawns and grass paths and a lot of the so-called island beds. It all faces north, and the underlying soil is a limey, inhospitable clay.

By the way, there are so many of these island and raised beds that my husband and I have found it a good plan to give them all names – the Boot Bed, Orion's Belt, the Barrett Border, and so on. This saves us a lot of tedious explanations when we are talking together about things in the garden and want to refer to a particular bed. I commend the idea to anybody with a large or even not large garden. We do not go so far as a man we knew who gave names to most of his garden tools and insisted that it saved him trouble. He had two wheelbarrows, for instance, that he called – believe it or not – Toots and Gongo!

If I ask myself what it is, apart from flowers, which I will come to later, that I most enjoy in November, I think the smells come first. I like the smell of rotting leaves, especially walnut leaves, a nice clean aromatic smell, and I like the pungent smell of newly-turned earth; but, most of all, I think I like the somehow nostalgic smell of a bonfire, never more than if it drifts in through an open window when I am snug in bed. And what fun it is *making* a bonfire. You should always be careful, when putting the material on to it, to lay any sticks parallel and never across each other. If you do not do this, they may not fall down as the fire burns, and then it will get a hole in it and may go out. And don't ever put on anything that can go on to the compost heap – which, by the way, will give you another smell, far from enjoyable, if it is not properly made.

After the smells come the colours: of the leaves first of all, mainly on the ground by the middle of the month, not as good as the October colours, of course, but by no means to be despised. We have a creeper, a vast *Celastrus orbiculatus*, climbing up and smothering an old thorn tree. It used to have lovely berries, but we never see one nowadays as the birds have learnt to eat the flower-buds in the spring; but in November, when its leaves fall, it produces a brilliant yellow carpet of leaves, thick and big enough to give us the rather childish fun of shuffling our feet in them. Not far off there is another yellow carpet – more feet shuffling – from a silver lime *(Tilia petiolaris)*. Then there is a white carpet – rather dingy I admit, and perhaps hardly worth mentioning – from a big old sorbus; and here and there little bright scarlet rugs under the Japanese maples.

Almost as enjoyable as the colours of the leaves and, of course, lasting much longer, are the colours of the barks, which you cannot really appreciate until the leaves are off. We grow a lot of willows especially for this: *Salix alba* 'Britzensis' for the red; 'Vitellina' for the yellow; and *S. daphnoides* for the white. I cannot think why everybody who has the space does not grow them; they are quite easy and don't need damp ground as so many people imagine. To get a good effect they should be planted in blocks, and are at their best on days when there has been a frost and the sun has come out and melted the ice on the long slender growths and made them all shiny. Our willows, which are quite old now, have four-foot trunks, and we cut the tops back hard every spring, as you only get the bright colours from the young growths.

The most noticeable bark of any tree in our garden is that of *Prunus serrula*, a brilliant glossy mahogany colour; near it is an *Acer griseum* which has a mahogany-coloured bark too, but paler and with a matt surface. We also have a lot of the so-called snake-bark maples, with barks of various shades of green veined with white. I think *Acer pensylvanicum* is the best of these, and we have a lovely form of this with bright red bark, 'Erythrocladum'. The trouble with these maples is that as they grow old the barks lose their distinctive colour and patterning. The brightest reds of all about now are the stems of a dogwood – the Westonbirt cornus; against a good background they are spectacular.

And I must not forget the evergreens. People often do not realise what a good colour green is, and how many different greens there are: from the yellowish-green of a griselinia to the dull dark green of the common yew – a tree that makes the perfect back-ground, and is not at all the slow grower it is often thought to be, *provided* you put the plants in quite small and give them a good start with compost round the roots.

I wish I could say some nice things about our coloured berries,

53 The brilliant glossy bark of *Prunus serrula* comes into its own during the winter months

too, but we have so many blackbirds and bullfinches, followed by flocks of voracious migrants, that they get gobbled up in no time, leaving us with nothing but some cotoneaster and berberis berries and here and there an inaccessible rose hip.

Another visual pleasure in November is being able to see the frameworks of the trees; they are well worth looking at. Things like prunuses and maples stretching up arms and fingers; parrotias pointing their horizontal branches like a lot of random signposts; ancient cotoneasters with their scrawny stems all criss-cross like streaks in an abstract picture; a willow, *Salix matsudana* 'Tortuosa' trying to look like one of the swirling trees that Van Gogh was so fond of painting; and the contorted hazel, or Harry Lauder's

Walking Stick (*Corylus avellana* 'Contorta'), looking like nothing on earth.

We get more than our fair share of fog and mists, and November is the time for them. Provided I do not have to go out on the roads, I don't mind them. They lend a touch of mystery to the garden and give me a lot of extra little things to wonder at: pearly drops on the edges of the leaves, or cobwebs all over the dwarf conifers and ericas, which make me realise what thousands and thousands of spiders there must be. And if there is a frost, I love looking at the patterns it makes on the glass of the frames.

And what a good, if strenuous, month November is in the vegetable garden. We make a great effort to have all the digging finished before the month is out. This is especially important on our heavy soil. The ground should be 'laid up', as they say, in big, fat, upstanding clods, for the frost and rain to get into it and break it down, so that when the time comes for spring sowing it can be raked into a fine tilth. This means manual spade work, as you can never get the same results with any kind of machine. I love digging, with my thirty-year-old stainless steel spade (perhaps it is even older than that, I cannot quite remember). It warms me up when I have a cold job to do, like tying climbers to the walls. The wooden part of my spade is painted white and so are the handles of all our tools. If a tool gets mislaid in a garden like ours it can easily be lost, but a white handle shows it up.

With luck everything should be looking tidy just now: the leeks in their trim military lines (I always try to plant them with the leaves parallel with the rows as this makes it so much easier to hoe them); the brussels sprouts, getting a bit bare below as they are picked, but still proud and pompous – no marauding pigeons yet; perhaps a row of red cabbage up against the brilliant white and green stems of some seakale beet; the sun shining on the upturned earth and, to go back to smells, the smell of celeriac roots as I lift them. Before the end of the month I hope to have tidied up all my small fruit, and by the end of the month, if my fingers do not get too frozen, I ought to have pretty well finished tying in my two

Morello cherry trees. Following the advice of an old gardener, I cut out as little as possible from them and never fail to get a heavy crop. There must be lots of north-facing walls just *asking* for a Morello cherry tree – lovely blossom, lovely fruit, lovely jam, and easy to grow.

But November can be quite a strenuous month apart from the vegetables and fruit. A flower garden needs constant replenishment, as Dean Hole once observed, however hardy the plants you grow (and no true gardeners confine themselves to completely hardy plants) and however carefully you look after them – and I, anyhow, never seem to have time to give my plants all the attention I know they ought to have. There will always be casualties and this means that I spend many hours in November taking the various steps needed to maintain a replacement stock for my shrub garden as well as for my raised beds. Shelters have to be devised for the less robust inhabitants – often a time-consuming operation – and a succession of cuttings have to be taken and plants lifted and transferred for winter into my greenhouse or frames. Things like cistus, ceanothus, olearias, some of the buddleias and a host of the little not so hardy or short-lived plants that beautify or add interest to my island and raised beds are constantly in my mind.

But enough of the toil and trouble and back to enjoyments and to thoughts of some of the flowers and foliage plants which stand out in November. Even before I leave the house I've been admiring a little shrub which has sent a branch across the window by my writing desk – *Correa backhousiana*. It has creamy-green tubular flowers and small felty green leaves; not spectacular perhaps, but it has a modest charm and can generally be relied on to keep flowering all winter. Another attraction just now on the wall of the house are the seed-heads of a particularly good form of the lemon-peel clematis – *C. orientalis* 'Bill Mackenzie'. A plant of it has rampaged all up the house outside the garden door and the glistening fuzzy seed-heads are lovely – almost best after dark if we turn on the porch light and it shines on them.

We follow the usual ritual of growing some hybrid tea and floribunda roses down by the house, and in a normal year (if there ever *is* such a thing), we can usually count on being able to pick a rose every day of the month, sometimes even till Christmas Day. The inevitable 'Iceberg' is among our most reliable contributors for this purpose, and in the last few years a rose, 'Ballerina', which has climbed quite high into the evergreen *Azara microphylla* on the wall (she isn't really supposed to climb) has occasionally surprised us with a bunch of her apple-blossom flowers quite late on. But November is quite definitely not the time for talking about roses.

Leaving the piece of garden by the house, we go up the steps, and beside them, on a series of little windswept north-facing terraces, are some of our best winter foliage plants – the celmisias; their shapely, stiff, pointed silver leaves seeming to sprout out of the ground and never losing their beauty the whole year through. Just now they are superb, contrasting with the dark-green, pink-stemmed marbled leaves of a special hardy strain of *Helleborus lividus*, which produces clusters of green flowers with the back of the petals a deeper pink; some are out already, and they will go on flowering till June. At the top of the steps we come to the oblong bit of the garden with its low stone walls and raised beds, which are made up, some with imported acid soil, the rest with my ordinary alkaline soil, and containing literally thousands of small hardy plants and bulbs. At the moment, in one of the north-facing acid beds, there is a gorgeous mat of the dark red autumn leaves of *Cornus canadensis*, through which are growing the last of some bright blue late-flowering gentians, 'Susan Jane' by name. Nearby are the long hanging tassels, a vivid pink, of *Polygonum amplexicaule* 'Arun Gem', a plant from Nepal which flowers until a bad frost comes.

On a neighbouring south wall there are still a lot of the eye-catching flowers of *Abutilon megapotamicum*, like tiny red and yellow paper lampshades tucked into each other; and, close by, that excellent architectural foliage plant, *Melianthus major*, with large handsome, almost blue, crinkled leaves. It dies down in the

54 Above: The flowers of *Abutilon megapotanicum* are like tiny red and yellow paper lampshades

55 *Melianthus major* with its large, handsome foliage

winter and I cover it with peat and compost. A few nerines are still out and the last of the white or pink daisy-like flowers of the dimorphothecas. Against another wall there's a splash of bright yellow from an excellent small shrub, *Coronilla valentina*. For some years now it has flowered all winter, and its pea-like flowers keep their lovely scent. It stays compact, unlike the more usually grown *Coronilla glauca*, which is liable to straggle and has a much shorter flowering season.

But it is the silver and golden foliage plants that really come into their own in the raised beds, now that they no longer have to compete with the bright colours of all the spring and summer flowers. I ought to explain that these beds – nearly two hundred yards of them (far too much really, but you just can't stop a garden expanding if you are a plant collector) – are about four feet wide and the height of two railway-sleepers on edge. This makes them less laborious to weed (hand-weeding, of course, on the knees, with the marvellous rubber knee-pads which we absolutely live in), and ensures good drainage. The plants are far easier to examine and enjoy too, especially the tiny alpine ones. Of the silver foliage plants, *Euryops acraeus* is one of the showiest. It is sometimes covered with yellow daisies in summer, but is well worth its place in the border for its foliage alone and it withstands the hardest of winters. Another good one is *Saxifraga longifolia*, which has big silvery rosettes; but nothing can surpass *Leucogenes grandiceps*, the New Zealand Edelweiss. Its tiny silver leaves positively shine.

56 The silver leaves of *Euryops acraeus*

Among the gold ones, *Thymus citriodorus* 'E. B. Anderson' has the merit of smelling delicious, and the yellow-leaved form of the common aubrieta makes a brave show. A taller plant, *Hebe armstrongii,* has golden whipcord stems and, by a lucky chance, a silver-leaved *Potentilla speciosa* has appeared, self-sown, at the foot of one of them. This potentilla was given to me by the late Walter Ingwersen years ago.

The other day, some visitors were rather amused by some black and brown plants, and I have now started talking about my Black and Brown Border. For the black I have *Cosmos atrosanguineus,* a sort of tiny dahlia, sometimes flowering until the middle of November and smelling like chocolate, reinforced by a strange

57 *Leucogenes grandiceps*

creature from Japan with a strange name, *Ophiopogon planiscapus* 'Nigrescens', a little thicket of narrow, iris-like, jet black leaves. My brown is provided by a diminutive *Gunnera hamiltonii*, most improbably related to the gigantic waterside one, with bronze leaves; backed up by a dwarf bronze New Zealand flax.

And now through the gate into 'the maze', the two acres of trees and shrubs and grass paths and lawns and island beds – and, thank goodness, no more mowing to worry about. In the island beds themselves, there is nothing particularly exciting left; just a few pleasing greens and browns, and the euphorbias – *wulfenii* especially, with great billowing masses of grey-green leaves – are a fine sight. But practically all the bright colours have gone. There may be a few patches of red from sedums; some pink and white from the last of the *Cyclamen hederifolium*; more pink from an occasional schizostylis and stray polygonums; some crimson from an *Erica carnea* just coming out; and spots of white from the very early, far *too* early, *reginae-olgae* snowdrops (I really don't know why I grow them. Quite a lot of people seem to like them but I much prefer my snowdrops at the right time of year and in great drifts). But if you look round, you will see the brilliant scarlet foliage of *Rosa virginiana* still blazing; the yellow of *Elaeagnus pungens* 'Maculata' shining more brightly than ever; *Spiraea prunifolia* managing to hang on to its tiny red leaves; and a promise of better things all over the place. The catkins of *Garrya elliptica* are forming; the buds show on *Sycopsis sinensis* (an excellent but seldom seen February-flowering small evergreen tree from China, bearing little red and yellow tassels like the parrotia ones); there are specks of yellow on some of the hamamelis buds; and the bushes of *Viburnum grandiflorum* are already plentifully sprinkled with pinkish-red corymbs (I think that is the correct word) of sweet-smelling flowers.

I must not let this piece turn into a recital of plant names, but I hope I have mentioned enough to show that a garden can be interesting in rather a dead month. I can think of several gardens well worth visiting even in late November, but I must admit that if I were walking round our garden with visitors just now my mind would probably be straying to the jobs I ought to be doing: cloche glasses that need cleaning, winter shelters I ought to be putting over my more tender treasures; leaf-mould and compost I ought to be spreading; and then all those tiresome leaves that keep falling from the lime trees on to one of the beds, which I ought to be raking off with my invaluable rubber rake.

Indeed, there are times when I begin to wonder if I am not *too* devoted to my garden, *too* impatient of interruptions, *too* content doing some perhaps quite inessential garden job, with my husband not far away, busy hand-weeding, my beloved pug dog beside me, and my favourite robin sitting expectantly on a neighbouring twig. But I do not really think I want to be any different.

DECEMBER

by

Roy Lancaster

A gardening acquaintance once confessed to me how he hated December – because it was cold and miserable and the soil wet and unworkable, and because nothing flowered or even grew. I regret to say that he was one of those tiresome fair-weather gardeners who flee indoors when it rains, observe their plants between ten o'clock in the morning and four o'clock in the afternoon and hibernate during winter.

To me rain adds a new dimension to the garden when previously dull or unassuming leaves gain a shine and a gleam to compete with those from more favourable climes. Barks, too, reveal hidden charms when coated with moisture, and I think especially of the snow gum *(Eucalyptus niphophila)* whose normally cream and grey pied bark reveals three or four extra shades when wetted by a storm. As for midday gardening, it is a fact well known to poets, painters, photographers and all true gardeners that the most satisfying, beautiful and breathtaking effects are most often seen at the beginning and the end of the day. Nor should we ignore the garden at night when, through the careful use of plain illumination or simply by means of a pocket flashlight, quite ordinary plants can take on new and exciting characters.

December, far from being miserable and motionless, can be a most happy time for the gardener, who, without the multitudinous distractions of flowering months, can organise his thoughts and actions and consider a few of the basics. With deciduous trees

59 One of the gums with interesting bark patterns – *Eucalyptus dalrympleana*

and shrubs naked, December is an excellent month to observe and enjoy the evergreens who, free from the overwhelming competition of summer, stand up to be counted and assessed for their ornamental value.

I suppose conifers claim the most attention with their enormous variety of shapes and colours. If we forget the ubiquitous Leyland cypress, which has revolutionised the hedging industry, I would put in a plea for the common arbor-vitae or western red cedar (*Thuja plicata*) which, in its form, 'Fastigiata', makes a splendid tall column of glistening green, sprayed foliage, requiring the minimum of clipping when used as a screen. I enjoy crushing its leaves and sniffing their distinctive aroma which always reminds me of those delicious pear-drop sweets I adored as a child.

If you have a garden which will accommodate large conifers, then I would certainly consider several of the pines, which, with few exceptions, are tough and adaptable. For cold or windswept places there is little to match the Japanese black pine *(Pinus thunbergii)*, which in its native isles grows on sand-dunes and sea cliffs, taking all that the elements can devise. Along the south and west coasts of the British Isles we should also consider the Monterey pine *(Pinus radiata)* of California whose grass-green young needles and squat limpet-like cones contrast effectively with the dark green needles and the longer cones of the other. Both these pines in the right situation make excellent windbreaks or screens. Talking of exposed gardens and pines, there are none more useful to such situations than *Pinus pumila* and *P. mugo* from Japan and Europe respectively. Both are dense bushy pines, ranging in height from two or three feet, to fifteen feet, and both are apt to cover extensive areas in their native mountains. The European one has green needles in pairs, while that from Japan has distinctive blue-green needles in bunches of five. Selected and sometimes named forms may be used in a wide range of difficult situations in the garden.

If blue is your favourite colour, then I would recommend the twenty-foot-plus cones of *Cupressus glabra* 'Pyramidalis', the Arizona cypress, which is as dense and as compact as anyone could wish. It is amenable to extremes of temperature and is a useful specimen tree for lawns, as long as one bears in mind the possible troubles from shallow rooting which is a family trait. Isolated specimens in exposed windswept situations are liable to lean, and may need the support of strong wires unless, of course, they are interplanted with other trees such as pines. Other blue cypresses belong to *Chamaecyparis* and include several fine Lawson forms, of which 'Pembury Blue' and 'Grayswood Pillar' are superb, the last named being the narrower of the two. Even narrower is the Juniper called 'Skyrocket', whose chimney-like spires are of a greyish-green and extremely effective when planted among lower growing, wide spreading junipers such as *Juniperus davurica* 'Parsonsii', *J. virginiana* 'Grey Owl' and *J.* × *media* 'Hetzii'.

For those with small gardens one of the most effective and satisfying arrangements can be achieved with the clever use of dwarf conifers. Several years ago, in the Hillier Arboretum, we had a particularly difficult slope on an acid Bagshot sand. We planted this with a combination of low growing or prostrate junipers, of which *Juniperus communis* 'Effusa' and 'Repanda' were the main components. These form very attractive, wide, low mounds of neat green foliage. To these we added the bronze-yellow *J. communis* 'Depressa Aurea', the apple-green prickly leaved *J. conferta*, and the grey-green waves of *J. sabina tamariscifolia*. To give height we planted a scattering of *J. communis* 'Compressa', whose tight grey-green columns, like miniature Irish junipers, gave the finishing touch to a most charming landscape, and all of it below knee level.

Of course there are lots of other dwarf conifers to choose from, and among my favourites is the American creeping juniper, *Juniperus horizontalis*, whose far-reaching stems can quickly cover bare ground to create quite startling carpets of blue or grey which, in some forms, assume plum-purple or metallic tints in winter. Two of the best forms are named 'Bar Harbor' and 'Marcellus'. Other reliable dwarf or slow-growing conifers worth considering are *Tsuga canadensis* 'Bennet'; *Cryptomeria japonica* 'Globosa'; *Pinus nigra* 'Hornibrookiana', *Pinus mugo* 'Mops'; *Picea abies* 'Echiniformis'; *Abies balsamea* 'Hudsonia'; *Thuja orientalis* 'Aurea Nana' and 'Conspicua' (both rich yellow); *Thuja occidentalis* 'Caespitosa'; *Chamaecyparis pisifera* 'Plumosa Compressa', *C. pisifera* 'Compacta', *C. pisifera* 'Golden Mop', *C. obtusa* 'Kosteri' and 'Nana Lutea', *C. lawsoniana* 'Pygmaea Argentea' and 'Minima Aurea'.

For those who like to try something a little more unusual I can recommend *Cedrus deodara* 'Golden Horizon', a lovely low mound of sulphur-yellow; *Cupressus sempervirens* 'Swane's Gold', which is a slow-growing golden form of the Italian cypress;

60 A view of the Hillier Arboretum showing *Erica mediterranea* 'W. T. Rackliff' *Erica carnea* 'Springwood Pink', *Erica* × *darleyensis* 'Arthur Johnson' and *Cupressus sempervirens* 'Stricta'

Sequoia sempervirens 'Prostrata', but make sure you prune out the strong occasional reversions; and, finally, *Microbiota decussata*. The last named is a low, flat-topped cypress-like conifer, which is native of a lonely, cold Siberian river valley to the east of Vladivostock. It has rather feathery, fresh green, leafy branches becoming bronzed in winter, and despite its rarity is quite easy to grow. On a recent visit to Boskoop, in Holland, I saw it in many gardens where it was commonly planted in association with other dwarf conifers and with heathers.

Mention of heathers, of course, reminds me of the superb effects one can achieve by planting the various types of heath and heather together with dwarf conifers. On acid soils it is possible to plant heathers for all-year-round flower effect, but on other soils, especially those of a limey nature, the winter-flowering kinds, mainly belonging to *Erica carnea*, *E. mediterranea*, and their hybrid, *Erica × darleyensis*, are excellent. For December flowering I would recommend *E. carnea* 'Praecox Rubra', with purple-red flowers, 'King George', purple-pink, and 'Snow Queen', white; while of the hybrids, *Erica × darleyensis*, 'Darley Dale', light purple-pink, and 'Silberschmelze', white, are more vigorous in growth.

Those who garden on acid soils can also plant some of the coloured foliage heathers, such as *Calluna vulgaris* 'Gold Haze' and 'Beoley Gold' – both yellow – and 'Sunset', a brilliant bronze-red. For contrast try 'Silver Queen', a striking silvery-grey form. Some gardeners prefer not to prune their heathers, which, as a result, increase in size until they eventually need replacing. Other pundits recommend pruning each year, usually after flowering, cutting away the old flowering shoots to encourage vigorous young growth.

The exciting peak of December, of course, is Christmas, and the two evergreens we most associate with this glad occasion are the holly and ivy. Everyone knows the English holly with its prickly leaves, but this is only one of over three hundred hollies from around the world. Some are very different indeed from our favourite, and I enjoy showing visitors to the Arboretum some of the most striking species such as the easy-to-grow *Ilex crenata*, with tiny box-like leaves, and the large-leaved *Ilex latifolia*, both from Japan. There is a Chinese deciduous holly tree called *Ilex macrocarpa*, which has fruits like black cherries; and the fiercely-spined Chinese *Ilex cornuta* makes a dense, exceedingly handsome mound, some six to eight feet high. Forms of the last include 'Burfordii', a free-fruiting, smooth-leaved bush up to three feet, and 'Rotunda', a strongly-armed, non-berrying kind which looks like a cross between a hedgehog and a football.

It is the English holly, though, which we prefer for the important task of hedging, and these are best planted when small, preferably in September or early October. The same can be said for almost all hardy evergreens grown in the open ground, although planting can be done throughout winter, while container-grown evergreens may be planted any time, as long as due attention is paid to after care, especially watering. When planting hollies as specimen trees in a border or lawn for ornamental effect, it pays to choose carefully. For a start, you must remember that, like willows and poplars, hollies carry their male and female parts in separate flowers on separate trees. To induce fruiting, therefore, you need both male and female hollies in reasonably close proximity to allow the early bees to play their essential part in the pollination. Most gardens can count on there being a male holly somewhere in the neighbourhood, but if there is one close to the female even better. One of the best free-flowering male hollies is called the hedgehog holly, *Ilex aquifolium* 'Ferox', a dense, slow-growing, bushy form with small leaves peppered with prickles; 'Ferox Argentea' has the leaves boldly marked creamy-white and is therefore better value. Of the many berrying forms, I can recommend the following: 'Amber' – green leaves, orange berries; 'Bacciflava' – green leaves, yellow berries; 'Pyramidalis' – green leaves, red berries; 'Handsworth New Silver' – creamy-white margined leaves, red berries; 'Madame Briot' – gold-margined leaves, red berries.

In recent years several of the so-called 'Victorian evergreens' have returned to favour. I have mentioned the holly, and another happens to be the ivy. Unlike the hollies, there is but a handful of wild ivies, of which the common ivy, *Hedera helix*, is the most usually grown. There are many attractive variations of this, some of which owe their popularity to their being used as houseplants. But they are hardy creepers, and perfectly suitable for all sorts of places in the garden – walls, tree-trunks, and ground-cover being a few – and, contrary to what is often said, ivy will not destroy a well-made wall nor a large healthy tree.

61 The tangled stems of a common ivy on an oak suggests those of a strangling fig from the tropics

I was recently married and my wife, Sue, and I moved into a new house on the chalk of Winchester. Amazingly the builders constructed a six foot red brick wall around part of our garden, and I immediately saw the potential of this splendid structure. Along the south-facing foot of the wall I planted a selection of unusual plants, many of them semi-hardy, donated by friends. One of my nursery friends, an ivy expert, very generously sent me a package of some six to eight cultivars to plant on the north-facing side of the wall. They included three of my favourites – the big, bold-leaved *Hedera colchica* 'Dentata', and the cream variegated 'Dentata Variegata', and *H. canariensis* 'Variegata', all of which, once established, give superb coverage to whatever you wish to conceal. They are particularly valuable for training up and over those nasty looking chain-link fences that builders use to separate properties on new estates. Among the other varieties there was a dwarf-spreading one with small, white-margined, diamond-shaped leaves, known as 'Little Diamond'. This also makes a lovely pot or rock-garden shrub. 'Ivalace' has attractive small, curly, green leaves, while 'Curly Locks' is a larger version. Both 'Curly Locks' and another, called 'Brocamp', colour a warm red-purple during winter, returning to green in spring.

I am often asked to recommend a shrub to plant in the garden where it can be seen from the kitchen window – a shrub which must have interest all the year round, but especially in winter. After careful thought, I suggest planting a *Mahonia*, such as 'Charity', 'Buckland', 'Lionel Fortescue' or 'Winter Sun'. These are evergreens of stately appearance with superb, bold, prickly leaves arranged in dense ruffs towards the ends of the erect stems. A well grown specimen may reach eight feet, but six feet is a good average. The attractive foliage is thoroughly acceptable throughout the year, especially when the coppery-purple young leaves appear in spring, but the most exciting time comes in late autumn, when the clear yellow, sweetly scented flowers appear in long, terminal, tapered racemes. I count them among my 'top ten' shrubs, growing as they do on almost all soils – chalk or acid.

Before leaving evergreens – and I have not even scratched the surface – I must tell you about one of my favourite groups of plants, the bamboos. They are, in fact, woody-stemmed grasses and are possessed of a wide range of ornamental as well as utilitarian qualities. Most of those grown in our gardens originate from Asia, especially China and Japan, where they are highly prized and used for all sorts of things. With few exceptions, the hardy bamboos are happy in ordinary soil and only actively dislike the extremes of dry and wet. In the great drought of 1976, for instance, many bamboos suffered severely, while some even perished.

I suppose bamboos can be divided into three main categories, depending on their habit of growth. First we have the tall-growing, ten-foot-plus kinds, with fast creeping rootstock. These spread like mad and are eminently suitable for wild places. Two of the wildest are *Phyllostachys flexuosa* and *Phyllostachys aurea*. They also include our two most commonly cultivated bamboos in *Arundinaria anceps* and *Arundinaria japonica*, both of which, by the way, make excellent dense screens. I might add that these vigorous thicket bamboos provide, when established, fascinating adventure areas for children, as long as they are made out of bounds during spring when the fragile young shoots are developing. The second big group are those tall growing bamboos, which do not run wild, and which form a dense clump suitable for a bed in the lawn or in the woodland garden. Four of the best for general planting are *Arundinaria murielae* and *A. nitida*, both of which dislike cold exposed places; *A. spathiflora* and *A. tessellata*. The last named, by the way, comes from South Africa and is the only hardy African bamboo. Its beautifully banded green and white canes were used by the Zulus to make their war shields.

The third category consists of the dwarf or low-growing bamboos, most of which are vigorous and thicket forming. One of my favourites is *Sasa veitchii*, up to three feet high, with bold leaves which take on a variegated appearance during winter. For the best results you should have a good clearout of your bamboo clump or thicket each or every other winter, when the old fading canes should be cut away clean from the base. These can be used in the garden for various purposes. A feed of general fertiliser in spring, and perhaps again in early autumn, is also beneficial and much appreciated.

I wonder how many plants you can think of which *flower* in December? Compared with other months they are few in number but, of course, all the more appreciated as a result. A particular favourite of mine is a deciduous shrub known as *Daphne bholua* 'Gurkha'. The type itself is found in the Himalaya, and I have seen it commonly in the mountains of Nepal. In 1962, a friend of mine, Major Tom Spring Smyth, collected three seedlings of this shrub at ten and a half thousand feet, on a ridge known as the Milke Banjgang in East Nepal. He gave them to a native porter who ran down the valleys to Dharan Bazaar, whence they were taken by jeep to Calcutta. From here they travelled via the diplomatic bag to the British Museum in London. Two of the seedlings were sent to the garden of Tom's parents in New Milton, Hampshire, where they were planted out. Eventually one died, but the other flourished and is now a six-foot-tall bush which, from December onwards, is a mass of sweetly-scented flowers which are white stained purple on the outside. It is to this seedling that the name, 'Gurkha' was specially given. It is reliable and vigorous for a *Daphne*, and for my money is one of the 'top ten' shrubs for the enthusiast's garden. By the way, it isn't very fussy about soil, as long as it is not waterlogged, and it will grow in sun or semi-shade.

It is stories like this that really make our gardens come alive and give to gardening a sense of adventure and romance. I travel to many countries in search of wild plants and, after the ultimate excitement of finding new plants, one of my greatest thrills is seeing plants with which I am familiar in cultivation. Old friends in their native habitats bring me a special kind of satisfaction which warms the cockles of my heart every time I meet them afterwards. I shall never forget having the honour and good fortune, one day, several years ago now, in conducting around the Arboretum the late Harold Comber who introduced many plants from the Andes of Chile and Argentina, and later from Tasmania. Every so often he would say to me, 'Did you see that tree waving at me?' or 'That flower winked at me!' He would then answer my bemusement by adding 'I introduced that in 1929', or 'I brought the seed home from Chile in my pyjama pocket', and so on. They were great characters, the old plant collectors, and I regret that we too often forget the troubles they went to in obtaining plants for our gardens: many of them risking and sometimes losing their lives for our benefit.

Combining winter flower with an evergreen nature is *Viburnum tinus*, a native of the Mediterranean region as you will soon realise if you try to grow it in a cold northern area. Even a severe southern winter will scorch its leaves but happily, or rather hopefully, this is an unusual event and the laurustinus remains one of the best of its kind. I have seen it planted as a hedge, and for this purpose choose one of the compact forms such as 'Eve Price' which has a neat habit and white flowers that are red in bud.

A nurseryman friend in Surrey once returned from a Christmas holiday in Spain full of praise for an evergreen *Clematis* he had seen scrambling through and over a roadside thicket. He showed me a photograph he had taken and the cream coloured, green washed, bell flowers took me back to my student days at the University Botanic Garden, Cambridge, where I first encountered *Clematis cirrhosa*. It is occasionally seen in gardens but not often enough, and looks best when trained 'au naturelle' through a deciduous shrub or hedge. A variety of this from the Balearic Isles – var. *balearica* – is possibly prettier with its much divided leaves, bronze-tinted in winter. This too I remember from Cambridge days and it seems altogether a more reliable plant, flowering more freely and over a longer period from autumn almost till spring.

Of other shrubs flowering in December, I would not be without the sweetly scented *Viburnum farreri*, or its hybrids, *V.* × *bodnantense* 'Dawn' and 'Deben'; nor would I forget the utterly reliable winter jasmine, *Jasminum nudiflorum*, with its cheerful yellow flowers. Yellow also is the chief contribution now of the Chinese witch hazel *Hamamelis mollis* with its amusing spidery flowers clustered along the naked branches. There are several excellent cultivars which however are later flowering, and if I were to choose just three I would plump for *Hamamelis mollis* 'Pallida' with large sulphur flowers, *H.* × *intermedia* 'Allgold', with deep yellow, almost amber flowers, and *H.* × *intermedia* 'Jelena', with flowers of a rich coppery-red. All make large shrubs with ascending and spreading branches, and although tolerant of chalk, they do best in a good acid to neutral loam.

All these flowering shrubs may be cut when in bud and displayed in the home, where they bring colour and cheer. Nor must we forget in this context our old friend, the Japanese autumn-flowering cherry, *Prunus subhirtella* 'Autumnalis', a small tree up to twenty-five feet, for any soil, with small white, or, in 'Autumnalis Rosea' blush flowers.

But let not this enthusiasm on the part of evergreens and winter flowers rob of us of the pleasure to be found in dead or dying foliage and herbaceous stems. I have never gone along with those gardeners who advocate a policy of tidiness at all times and in all places, who see winter's arrival as a signal for systematic removal of all spent growth. Clear away drifted debris by all means but please, before wielding secateurs, knife or shears, pause and consider your intended victim with an artist's eye. Think on those countless paintings one sees of wintry landscapes where foreground interest and beauty is provided by the sundry hoary outlines of dead herbage – the silver-margined bramble, the spangled hogweed and the frosted teasel. These effects are multiplied and diversified in gardens where the growths of summer are allowed to remain until spring. In such gardens I have seen the skeletons of *Astilbe, Iris, Dierama, Watsonia, Verbascum, Eryngium, Limonium, Sedum* and many others become transformed by the whims of rain, frost or snow, adding a new exciting dimension to our enjoyment and appreciation. Just as the current wave of vegetable mania has alerted people to the importance of utilising every inch of ground, let us also consider and exploit the full potential of our ornamental plants.

Colourful shoots are such an integral part of the December scene that at the risk of touching on what others may have advised, I shall mention a few of the less familiar.

Shrubs with bark which shreds or peels away to hang in strings or tatters have always attracted me. There are several deutzias such as *D. compacta* and *D. pulchra* which have this propensity and look most effective throughout winter when the grey-brown old bark strips to reveal the rich orange-brown interior. These two sucker

62 *Acer griseum* with its rich cinnamon bark is one of the best Chinese trees introduced by E. H. Wilson

quite freely and when these are carefully severed and lifted provide ideal presents for gardening friends.

Some of the daisy bushes – *Olearia species* – shed their bark when mature and I can recommend *O. macrodonta* and the rare *O. lacunosa*, old specimens of which have long streamers blowing in the wind. The latter species is somewhat more tender and I recall a magnificent old specimen at Wakehurst Place which always reminded me of a tramp with incredibly torn and tattered garments.

Those of you who are lucky enough to garden in the milder south-western regions of the British Isles should be aware of *Fuchsia excortica* from New Zealand. Unlike its South American cousin – *F. magellanica* – and its hybrids, it is no beauty in flower but partly makes up for this in its grey-shaded reddish bark which peels and flakes in a most attractive manner. It can and does make a small tree in sheltered gardens and a little judicial pruning will help the stems to carry their charm well up above one's head.

Few ornamental fruits retain their colour and prestige beyond Christmas and those which do are worth remembering for future reference. Several cotoneasters manage it including the ubiquitous *Cotoneaster horizontalis*, whose herring-bone branches are so often crucified against a wall that an acquaintance of mine, a bit of a wag, once gave seed of such a plant to a persistent scrounger telling him that it was a new species called *C. verticalis*. I later heard that the recipient, having grown several plants, could not understand why their branches grew horizontally. He once again approached the donor who confided in him that in the wild the shrub grew up cliffs and rock faces and in cultivation, therefore, it was necessary to build it a supporting wall. I never did hear whether the wall was built.

The big bold hybrids of *C. frigidus* and *C. salicifolius* keep their fruits, and for the large garden or wild area these are useful first plantings especially if the yellow fruited cultivars such as 'Exburyensis' and 'Rothschildianus' are mixed with the reds of 'Cornubia' and 'St Monica'. Ask at your local garden centre for the name of a winter-berrying shrub and nine times out of ten the

word firethorn will be trotted out, which is fair enough considering the long lasting and colourful qualities of these evergreen
shrubs. Of late the name firethorn has been uncomfortably paired
with that of fireblight, which disease is prevalent in some areas and
damaging to members of Rosaceae to which *Pyracantha* belongs.
Outbreaks are scattered however and there is no immediate
danger to those countless representatives of this group on sub-
urban walls and trellises throughout the British Isles.

Of the several cultivars currently available I would recommend
the following: 'Golden Charmer' – large orange-yellow fruits;
'Orange Charmer' – large orange-red fruits; 'Orange Glow' –
deep orange fruits; *rogersiana* 'Flava' – bright yellow fruits; *coccinea*
'Lalandei' – large orange-red fruits.

Now is a good time to plant deciduous trees and shrubs, and I
sincerely believe that a liberal helping of well-rotted manure or
compost in the planting hole is far more beneficial than a spadeful
of peat. In the Arboretum we always add a handful of slow-release
fertiliser to each hole before planting, while, as a boost to jaded
trees and shrubs, a similar dose of nitro-chalk can work wonders
when forked into the soil surface in spring.

The planting site should have been carefully chosen and prepared beforehand, so that when the tree arrives, weather per-
mitting, it can be planted without delay. If it is a standard tree with
a five- to six-foot clear stem, then a stake will be required: order
this with the tree. The hole is dug deep enough and wide enough
to accommodate the roots without bending or breaking. The
stake is positioned and the base hammered firmly into the bottom
of the hole. The tree is then carefully planted, treading each
spadeful of soil firmly. The stem is attached to the stake by means
of special rubber tree-ties, and *not* by string, rag, rope, or nylon
stockings. After-care is as important as planting, and each year ties
must be checked and loosened if necessary, and both watering and
mulching carried out to prevent the roots from drying out,
especially during the summer.

Because I am the curator of an arboretum, I am often regarded as a tree man, as if I had no interest in other plants. I must admit now that I have never been able to wear blinkers and devote myself exclusively to any one group. Life is too short, and there are so many interesting plants to be seen and grown. The ferns are a good example. There is an incredible array of ferns growing in the world and, even forgetting the tropical ones, there are plenty left to fill our gardens. Even in December ferns play a part in the garden scene, and I am thinking especially of the so-called hard ferns, *Blechnum* species. *Blechnum chilense* is big and bold with arching, leathery, dark-green fingered fronds up to three feet. It is very happy in moist soil, forming large colonies in sun or shade; *B. penna-marina* from New Zealand, by comparison, is a diminutive fern, its short fronds forming dense carpets in shady peat or woodland gardens. Our own native hard fern, *B. spicant*, is somewhere in between these two and is a familiar fern of moors, heaths and woodlands, especially on acid soils. I always remember its dense clumps of glossy laddered fronds on Pennine banks, with purple moor grass, cobwebs, December mists, and rose heps gleaming like dragons' eyes in the hedgerow.

One of my favourite colour transparencies depicts a fruiting stem of the winter cherry or Chinese lantern – *Physalis alkekengii*. This rampant oriental is well worth its keep so long as it is planted in isolation away from lesser fry.

The orange bladders of autumn are instantly noticeable and near-luminous in certain lights but often attract scorn from gardening pundits of more subtle tastes. The pundits change their tune, and the *Physalis* its appearance, in winter, however, when the outer skin gnawed away by wind and frost reveals a skeletal cage of such delicacy that in close-up the reticulated framework has all the appearance of gold thread, a fitting repository for the bright red fruit within. Space prevents me from exploring the whole catalogue of effects which make the garden now so precious. Dull December – was ever a month so maligned?

THE
CONTRIBUTORS

Anne Scott-James had her first small garden plot at school and has been a devoted gardener ever since, with a cottage garden on the Berkshire downs. Well-known as a Fleet Street columnist and broadcaster, she began writing on gardening in 1968 for *Queen* Magazine. She has written three gardening books, *Down to Earth, Sissinghurst – the Making of a Garden*, and *The Pleasure Garden*, in collaboration with her husband, Osbert Lancaster.

Alan Bloom, with paternal encouragement, began gardening over sixty years ago, and at twenty-four had his own Nursery near Cambridge. He also became a farmer by 1938, undertaking extensive wartime land reclamation. He moved to Bressingham in 1946, but progress there was handicapped until after 1952, since when acreage has been doubled into a six-acre garden. He has had some twenty books published and has been awarded the Victoria Medal of Honour by the RHS. One hobby – steam engines – has led to the most comprehensive live museum in Britain. Both gardens and museum at Bressingham Hall, Norfolk, are open to the public about fifty afternoons from May to September inclusive.

After lecturing in Essex, **John Sales** joined the National Trust as assistant to Graham Thomas in 1971. In 1974 he succeeded as Gardens Adviser responsible for advice in over a hundred historic gardens throughout Britain, except in Scotland. He lectures frequently, is General Editor of Batsford's *Gardens of Britain* series and is writing the volume covering Glos., Wilts., Somerset and Avon. When home and with help from his wife and three sons he cultivates half an acre in Cirencester.

Garden writer, photographer and designer, **Peter Coats** has produced several garden books which have been best sellers, including *Flowers in History, Garden Decoration* and his autobiography *Of Generals and Gardens* and a book on the gardens of Buckingham Palace. For many years he has been garden Editor of *House and Garden* magazine.

'I equally enjoy,' says Mr Coats 'making large or small gardens. With thousands of pounds I can have a lot of fun – with twenty or thirty I have a challenge. I have planned gardens for Swiss tycoons, for many so-called stately homes, but also, for many young couples with simple back yards: and I have advised on a garden of scented plants for the blind.'

Christopher Lloyd was born at Great Dixter in 1921 and has lived there off and on ever since. After taking a horticultural degree at Wye College (University of London) 1950 and teaching there till 1954, returned to Dixter to look after the gardens and start a plant nursery. He was awarded the Victoria Medal of Honour by the RHS in 1979. Took to writing books (e.g. *The Well-Tempered Garden*) and articles – he has contributed weekly to *Country Life* since 1963. The gardens are open to the public daily, Mondays excepted, 2.00 to 5.00 p.m. April to mid-October.

Hugh Johnson is Editorial Director of *The Garden*, the journal of The Royal Horticultural Society, and author of *The Principles of Gardening, The International Book of Trees, The World Atlas of Wine* and other books. His own garden, Saling Hall, near Braintree, Essex, is open from time to time in summer or at any time for keen gardeners by appointment.

Lanning Roper is an American and a graduate of Harvard University. Even as a child he had a passion for flowers and gardens. As a US Naval Officer he participated in operations off Omaha Beach on D-Day, and later was happily stationed at Exbury.

After training as a student at Kew and the Edinburgh Botanic Garden he became assistant to the Editor of the RHS, but left to work as a landscape consultant and designer in this country and abroad.

For thirteen years he was Gardening Correspondent for *The Sunday Times* and is a contributor to *Country Life* and other publications. His books include *Successful Town Gardening*, *The Gardens in the Royal Parks at Windsor* and *The Sunday Times Gardening Book*. He always says, 'I am a peasant at heart. I like to dig in the soil and handle plants.'

Beth Chatto was born in Essex and trained as a teacher specialising in horticulture. Otherwise she has no formal training. After her marriage to an Essex fruit-grower she took an active interest in growing fruit. When she became the friend of the famous artist and plant-breeder, Sir Cedric Morris, with his large collection of plants she taught herself to propagate and grow an enormous range of plants.

She began her present garden at Elmstead Market, Colchester twenty years ago, converting four acres of wasteland into a very varied landscaped garden. The thriving nursery adjoining has been developed over the last ten years. Both open daily except Sundays and Bank Holidays.

As well as showing at Chelsea where she has won four Gold Medals, she has written *The Dry Garden*.

Graham Stuart Thomas is Gardens consultant to the National Trust and is noted for his collection of old roses, now housed at Mottisfont Abbey, Hants (National Trust). He is the author of

three books on Old Roses, also of *Colour in the Winter Garden,
Plants for Ground Cover, Perennial Garden Plants* and *Gardens of
the National Trust*. He is an artist, photographer and lecturer.
Awarded OBE for his work with the National Trust; Victoria
Medal of Honour by Royal Horticultural Society; Dean Hole
Medal by Royal National Rose Society.

Wilfrid Blunt – formerly schoolmaster, singer, and now curator
of the Watts Gallery at Compton, near Guildford – is the author of
many books on a variety of subjects including flowers. His *Art of
Botanical Illustration*, a standard work, is temporarily out of print
but should be available again shortly. Frances Lincoln, Publishers,
have just issued *The Illustrated Herbal*, which he has written in
conjunction with Sandra Raphael.

Valerie Finnis has gardened all her life. She holds the Royal
Horticultural Society's Victoria Medal of Honour and is on various committees of the Society, is widely known as a flower
photographer and has had successful exhibitions of her abstract
paintings. She gardens with her husband at Boughton House, near
Kettering, where they grow a wide range of plants. The garden is
open occasionally in aid of the National Gardens Scheme.

Roy Lancaster has been Curator of the Hillier Arboretum in
Hampshire since 1970 though he first joined the Hillier Nurseries
in 1962 after two years as a student at the University Botanic
Garden, Cambridge. The Arboretum is now in the care of Hampshire County Council and is open during the week from 9 a.m.
until 4.30 p.m. and on Sundays between Easter and the end of
October from 10 a.m. until 5 p.m. It contains one of the largest
collections of hardy woody plants in Europe.

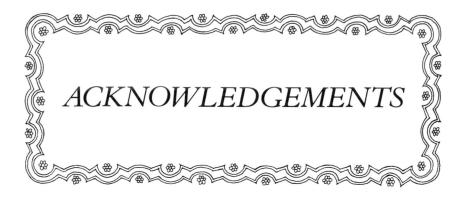

ACKNOWLEDGEMENTS

The publishers would like to thank Pamela Howe, Elspeth Napier and Anthony Huxley for their invaluable help and assistance in preparing this book.

The illustrations are copyright as follows: nos 1, 2, 7, 59, 60, 61, 62 and colour nos 3 and 24 © Michael Warren AIIP; nos 48, 51 and colour no. 19 © Wilfrid Blunt; nos 3, 4, 6 and colour nos 1 and 2 © Terry Hardman; colour nos 8 and 9 © Christopher Lloyd; nos 8 and 10 © Alan Bloom; no. 9 *Eastern Daily Press*; nos 16, 18 and colour no. 7 © Peter Coats; no. 58 and colour no. 23 © Roy Lancaster; nos 11, 13, 19, 20, 22, 23, 27, 28, 29, 30, 31, 34, 37, 38, 39, 40, 41, 42, 49, 50 and colour nos 5, 10, 11, 13, 14, 15, 16, 17 and 20 © the Harry Smith Horticultural Photographic Collection; no. 12 © The National Trust; no. 14 and colour no. 4 © John Sales; no. 35 © *Country Life*; nos 15, 17, 21, 36, 43, 44, 47, 52, 53, 54, 55, 56, 57 and colour nos 6, 12, 18, 21 and 22 © Valerie Finnis; nos 45 and 46 © G. S. Thomas; nos 24, 25 and 26 © Pat Brindley; nos 32 and 33 © Jonathan M. Gibson.